D1648573

Michigan Cooking

...and other things

by: Carole Eberly

Cover and Illustrations by William Kelley

eberly press

1004 Michigan Ave.
E. Lansing, MI 48823

ISBN 0-932296-00-9

Lighthouse at Point Betsie

A NOTE

Although Michigan is synonymous with automobiles, agriculture occupies the number two spot
in the state's industrial scheme. Michigan's
cornucopia is loaded with everything from asparagus,
cherries and popcorn to mushrooms, soybeans and
zucchini.

All the recipes in this book are based on the
state's agricultural products. Most are good old
favorites--Old Fashioned Apple Butter, Sourdough
Starter and Bread, Michigan Baked Beans--but there
are a few new recipes--Zucchini Bread, Soybean
Lemon Sponge Cake--and a few strange ones--Roast
Bear Paws, Asparagus Cookies.

But, if you like to cook and eat--and don't
mind learning a little about Michigan at the same
time--read on.

*   *   *

ACKNOWLEDGMENTS

Special appreciation goes to Michigan writers Robert Clock and Al Barnes for giving me permission to include their entertaining works. In addition, I wish to thank Mrs. Martha Sintz for letting me reprint an excerpt from a book written by her grandfather, Lewis C. Reimann.

*   *   *

CONTENTS

Grand Hotel, Mackinac Island

Martha-Mary Chapel, Greenfield Village

appetizers

snacks

beverages

PINCONNING CHEESE SPREAD

3/4 c. mayonnaise
1/4 c. pickle juice
1 lb. Pinconning cheese,
  grated

2 Tbsp. onions, minced
1/2 tsp. celery salt
1/4 c. pimiento, chopped

Place all ingredients, except pimientos, in blender and whirl until well mixed. Stir in pimientos. Spread on crackers or use as a sandwich spread. Makes about 3 cups.

*

COTTAGE CHEESE DIP

2 c. cottage cheese
1 green onion, chopped

1/2 tsp. garlic salt
1/8 tsp. Tabasco

Put all ingredients in blender and cream until smooth. Chill. Serve with fresh vegetable strips. Makes 2 cups.

*

SOYBEAN NUTS

1 c. dry soybeans
3 c. water

1 qt. salad oil
Salt

Soak soybeans overnight in water. Drain thoroughly. Spread on paper towels and allow to dry 1 hour. Heat oil in deep saucepan to 350 degrees. Put 1 cup of beans into fryer basket and lower slowly into oil. Fry about 6-8 minutes, or until crisp and lightly browned. Drain on paper towels. Fry remaining beans and drain. Sprinkle with salt. Makes about 2 cups.

*

ROAST PUMPKIN SEEDS

1/2 lb. pumpkin seeds   1 Tbsp. salt
1 Tbsp. salad oil

Spread seeds in shallow pan and roast at 300 degrees for 10 minutes. Sprinkle with oil and salt, mixing well. Roast, stirring often, for 30 more minutes.

*

SOFT PRETZELS

1-3/4 c. warm water   3 Tbsp. salad oil
1 pkg. dry yeast   5 c. unbleached flour
1 tsp. sugar   1 egg
2 tsp. salt   1/4 c. coarse salt

Sprinkle yeast over warm water in large bowl. Stir and let stand for 2-3 minutes. Add sugar, salt, oil and 3 cups flour, beating until smooth. Mix in 1 1/2 cups more flour. Turn out on surface floured with remaining 1/2 cup flour and knead 8-10 minutes or until dough is springy. Place in greased bowl, turning once to grease top. Cover with a towel and let rise in warm place for 1 hour. Punch down. Form into a ball and cut in half. Put half back into bowl and cover. Take other half and cut into 8 pieces. Roll a piece of dough with hands into a 20-inch rope, stretching occasionally. Lay the rope on floured surface and tie into a pretzel shape or a loose knot. Pinch the center together lightly. Continue with other 7 pretzels. Place on a large lightly greased baking sheet about 1 inch apart. Beat egg and brush on top of pretzels. Sprinkle with salt. Set in warm place to rise 15-20 minutes. Cut remaining dough into 8 pieces and make pretzels. Bake first batch of pretzels at 400 degrees for 15-18 minutes while second batch is rising. Serve warm with prepared mustard. Makes 16.

*

POPCORN

Popcorn has been first in the hearts of American nibblers since the Indians showed up with this treat at the Pilgrims' first Thanksgiving.

Michigan grows enough of it every year to bury a small town--a fact popcorn addicts are grateful for.

Popcorn connoisseurs keep their kernels in tightly sealed jars to keep insects out and moisture in. It's the lack of moisture in a kernel that keeps it from popping. If this happens to your kernels, sprinkle a little water in the jar, tighten the cap and shake it around until the kernels are evenly moistened. Let it stand a few hours and it'll be ready to go.

Popcorn pops, by the way, because the exceptionally dense texture and tough skin of the kernel holds the moisture in, turning it to steam when the heat is turned on. When the steam pressure builds up inside the kernel, it has no place to go and so it pops, exploding the kernel from 30-40 times its original size.

Popcorn is a favorite of dieters because 2 cups of it contain only 110 calories and yet is rich with vitamins and minerals.

So pop away and enjoy!

SEASONED POPCORN

2 1/2 qt. popped corn	1/2 tsp. garlic salt
(5 Tbsp. unpopped)	1 tsp. seasoned salt
1/2 c. melted butter	1/2 tsp. hickory smoked
1 pkg. onion soup mix	salt

Put popcorn in large bowl. Stir remaining ingredients together and pour over popcorn.

*

CARMEL CORN & NUTS

4 qt. popped corn
2 c. peanuts
1 c. butter
2 c. brown sugar

1/2 c. dark molasses
1 tsp. salt
2 Tbsp. water

Mix popcorn and nuts in roasting pan. In medium saucepan, melt butter. Stir in remaining ingredients. Cook over medium heat until boiling, stirring constantly. Boil to hard crack stage (290 degrees). Pour over popcorn mixture, stirring to coat.. Bake at 250 degrees for 20 minutes. Cool. Break into chunks.

*

SPICY POPCORN SNACK

3/4 c. butter
1 1/2 tsp. garlic salt
2 Tbsp. Worcestershire
   sauce

1/4 tsp. Tabasco
4 qt. popped corn
3 c. small pretzels
3 c. peanuts

Melt butter in small saucepan and stir in seasonings. Mix popcorn, pretzels and nuts in roaster. Pour butter mixture over all. Bake at 250 degrees for 30 minutes, stirring occasionally.

*

POPCORN STUFFING

1 large turkey

5 c. unpopped popcorn

Prepare turkey for roasting. Stuff popcorn inside and sew it up. Put in oven at highest heat. When the first kernels begin popping, get out of the kitchen. When turkey explodes, return to kitchen and clean up the mess. (Hopefully, no one would be tempted to try this old joke!)

HOT BUTTERED CIDER

1 gallon apple cider   1 stick cinnamon
1 c. brown sugar   2 tsp. whole cloves
1/2 c. butter

    Bring cider to a boil. Add remaining ingredients and simmer over low heat, stirring until sugar dissolves. Strain. Serves 16.

*

EGGNOG

6 eggs   2 Tbsp. vanilla extract
1 qt. milk   1/4 tsp. salt
2/3 c. sugar   Nutmeg

    Beat eggs until thick. Add rest of ingredients and mix until well blended. Serve topped with nutmeg. Makes 12 servings.

*

HONEY MILK DRINK

4 c. cold milk   1/8 tsp. nutmeg
3 Tbsp. honey   Dash salt

    Place all ingredients in blender and whirl at high speed for 20 seconds. Serves 4. (Add fruit or chocolate for variety.)

*

FRUIT MILKSHAKE

1 c. milk   3 Tbsp. fruit jam
1 scoop ice cream

    Put all ingredients in blender and whirl at high speed for 20 seconds. Serves 1.

*

CHERRY BOUNCE

2 qt. tart cherries   2 fifths whiskey
2 lb. sugar

Mix all ingredients together in a large jar or crock. Cover. Stir once a day for the first week. Stir once a week thereafter. Strain and bottle anytime after 2 months. Makes about 2 quarts.

*

PLUM CORDIAL

3 lb. purple plums,   1 stick cinnamon
   pitted & quartered   6 whole cloves
2 1/2 c. sugar   1 qt. bourbon
4 strips lemon peel

Combine all ingredients in a gallon jar. Cover. Stir daily for one week. Stir once a week there-after. Strain and bottle after 3 months. Makes 1 1/2 quarts.

*

CHERRY PICKING IN TRAVERSE CITY
(From Clockwise)*

by Robert Clock

If I were 18 years old and didn't have 17 children (there's only one but she eats like the Russian army), I'd be tempted to hire myself out as a picker in the Traverse City cherry country.

That's what I did the summer I was 18, and even today that July stands out among all the rest. I can still taste the tart fruit and feel the hot sun on the back of my neck as I stood on a three-legged ladder high in a Montmorency cherry tree.

I had never been to Traverse City before, but even down in Detroit folks were talking about the high wages being paid in the cherry orchards. Twenty-five cents a lug (25 lbs.) and all you could eat.

About mid-July I packed a wool Navy blanket, a pup tent and some old work clothes in my father's World War I sea bag, got him to drive me out to Woodward and Eight Mile Road and started hitchhiking north. Late that evening I walked the last mile into Traverse City, marched straight down to Grand Traverse Bay, slipped into my swimming trunks behind a bush and went for a long, cool swim. It had been a long, hot day on the road.

After dining on hamburgers, I asked a policeman how a fellow went about getting work in one of the orchards. I had gone to the right man. Together we walked over to the police station where several transients like myself were waiting for transportation out to a government-operated labor camp.

---

*Clockwise is an award-winning column written by Mr. Clock, a veteran newspaperman. This particular column appeared in the Charlevoix Courier in 1966 when he was editor of the newspaper.

Fortunately, transportation wasn't available immediately and we got to hang around the station all evening, listening to police calls and watching as officers disposed of one miscreant after another. Late in the evening, a lady of the streets was brought in kicking, screaming and dragging her heels as the police hauled her by the elbows into the station house. She swore and spit and called all of us every name in the book. It was so interesting I thought it might be fun to move to Traverse City permanently.

Finally, a police wagon pulled up and all the prospective cherry pickers were herded aboard for the ride out to the labor camp on U.S. 31 south of the city.

Although I had just finished reading John Steinbeck's "Grapes of Wrath," I wasn't quite prepared to find a full-fledged transient labor camp in Michigan. Surplus army squad tents were arranged in a semi-circle behind a clapboard administration building. We filed inside and the man on duty assigned each of us a tent number and asked if we'd like to pay 50 cents for the night or help police up the place in the morning. We all said we'd help police up.

The tents were equipped with cots and army blankets. Two boys from Atlanta and I were assigned to the same tent, and it wasn't long before we were fast asleep. In the morning we were awakened by the spicy aroma of Mexican food cooking over open fires. I was surprised to find that most of our fellow pickers were either from Texas or Mexico. Many spoke no English at all.

By mid-morning, the first call for workers came in. Three pickers were needed at the Thompson farm near Chum's Corners, the present junction of U.S. 31 and M-37.

My buddies from Atlanta and I jumped at the chance and within an hour we had hitchhiked to the Thompson place and pitched our pup tents on the Thompson's spacious front lawn.

The actual cherry picking wasn't too difficult, although we worked from sunup until near dusk. It was sort of like golf--trying every day to beat your previous record. Like any repetitive job, it lent itself well to daydreaming and constructive thinking. Sometimes you wouldn't see another picker in your section of the orchard for hours on end.

Evenings at Chum's Corners were pleasant. I usually fixed my supper over a little bonfire down by the road, then, ignoring everything I had learned about eating and swimming, I would hurry over to beautiful little Silver Lake for a bath and a swim. The area around the lake was a virtual wilderness at that time, so no bathing suit was called for.

Later, back at the Thompson's, I'd walk up the hill to talk to the other pickers--old Mr. Honeycutt from Arkansas who came up to Michigan every summer to pick cherries and a young couple from the Thumb area. Mr. Honeycutt stayed in a make-shift house-trailer, while the young couple bedded down in an abandoned hen house. Sometimes Mr. Thompson would visit with us and tell us about the winter he skated across Lake Michigan.

Every evening, on a high ridge opposite the orchard, a solitary farmer walked slowly back and forth behind his horse-drawn plow. Mr. Honeycutt and I used to speculate about why he was plowing in the dead of summer, but we never crossed the valley and climbed the hill to find out. We both agreed, however, that the farmer and his horse, silhouetted against the dying sun, made one of the prettiest pictures we had ever seen.

No doubt about it. If I were 18, there's no question which way I'd head this summer.

*   *   *

pickles

jams

sauces

DILL PICKLES

20-25 4-inch cucumbers
8 cloves garlic
24 heads dill
3 Tbsp. mustard seed

1 qt. cider vinegar
3 qt. water
1 c. coarse salt
Alum

Place cucumbers in 8 hot, sterile quart jars. Divide up next three ingredients and put in each jar. Boil vinegar, water and salt. Pour in jars. Add a pinch of alum to each jar. Seal. Makes 8 quarts.

*

CAULIFLOWER MUSTARD PICKLES

2 Tbsp. flour
1/2 tsp. dry mustard
1/4 tsp. tumeric
1 c. cold water
1/2 c. sugar
1/3 c. cider vinegar
2 tsp. salt
1/2 tsp. celery seed

1/8 tsp. garlic powder
1/2 tsp. mustard seed
1/8 tsp. Tabasco
2 c. small raw cauliflower
   flowerets
1/2 c. onion, sliced thin
1/4 c. green peppers,
   sliced thin

In a saucepan, mix together flour, mustard and tumeric. Gradually add in water while cooking over low heat and stirring constantly. When thickened, add in sugar, vinegar, salt, celery seed, garlic powder, mustard seed and Tabasco. Add cauliflower and onions. Cook for 2 minutes. Stir in green pepper, mixing well. Ladle into hot, sterile jars and seal. Makes 2 pints.

*

PICKLED GREEN BEANS

2 c. whole green beans,
  cooked
1 c. cider vinegar
1 c. sugar

1 c. water
1/8 tsp. garlic powder
1/8 tsp. salt

    Place beans in a sterile pint jar. Boil remaining ingredients and pour over beans. Seal. Makes 1 pint.

*

SWEET AND SOUR PICKLES

10 large cucumbers, sliced
5 large onions, sliced
1/2 c. coarse salt
1 pt. cider vinegar
1 c. brown sugar
1/2 tsp. turmeric

1 tsp. cinnamon
1 tsp. ginger
1/4 tsp. cloves
1 tsp. celery salt
2 tsp. mustard seed
1 tsp. pepper

    Mix cucumbers and onions in a large pot. Sprinkle with salt. Cover and let stand 1 hour. Drain. Add remaining ingredients and bring to a boil. Seal in hot, sterile jars. Makes 6 pints.

*

SWEET PICKLES

1 1/2 c. sugar
1 c. cider vinegar
2 Tbsp. salt
1 Tbsp. mustard seed

1 tsp. celery seed
1/2 tsp. cinnamon
2 qt. cucumbers, sliced
Alum

    Mix sugar and spices together in pot. Heat until sugar dissolves. Stir in cucumbers and cook 5 minutes. Pack in hot, sterile jars with a pinch of alum in each. Makes 3 pints.

*

PICKLED PUMPKIN

6 lbs. pumpkin
4 c. cider vinegar
4 c. sugar

2 c. water
18 cinnamon sticks
6 whole cloves

Peel pumpkin and cut into 1-inch cubes. Place in saucepan and cover with water. Simmer until tender, about 20 minutes. Drain. In the same saucepan, cover pumpkin and vinegar, sugar and water. Bring to a boil while stirring to dissolve sugar. Pack in hot sterile pint jars with 3 cinnamon stocks and a whole clove in each. Seal and process. Makes 6 pints.

*

PICKLED CARROTS

1 lb. carrots, cut
   into 1/4-inch pieces
1 c. sugar
1 1/2 c. white vinegar

1/2 c. water
3 Tbsp. mixed pickling
   spices

Cook carrots in salted water until crispy-tender, about 10 minutes. Drain. Mix remaining ingredients in saucepan and simmer for 10 minutes. Strain. Pour over carrots and boil for 2 minutes. Pack in hot, sterile jars. Seal and process. Makes about 2 pints.

*

PICKLED PEPPERS

5 c. cider vinegar
1 c. water

1 clove garlic
2 qt. green peppers

Combine vinegar, water and garlic in saucepan. Bring to a boil. Reduce heat and simmer uncovered 15 minutes. Remove garlic. Cut peppers into strips and pack in hot, sterile jars. Pour hot liquid over peppers. Seal and process. Let stand 2 weeks before serving. Makes 4 pints.

*

CORN RELISH

2 cucumbers	1 qt. vinegar
2 tomatoes	1 1/2 c. sugar
2 onions	1 Tbsp. salt
2 green peppers	1 1/2 Tbsp. dry mustard
6 c. cooked corn	1 tsp. turmeric

Peel and coarsely chop cucumbers, onions, tomatoes and peppers. Mix corn in with other vegetables. In a large saucepan, mix vinegar, sugar, salt, mustard and turmeric and heat to boiling. Add vegetables and boil until tender, about 20-30 minutes. Stir frequently. Pour into hot sterile jars and seal. Makes about 5 pints.

*

CHILI SAUCE

12 tomatoes	1 tsp. Tabasco
3 onions	1 Tbsp. salt
2 green peppers	1/2 tsp. ginger
1 pt. cider vinegar	1/2 tsp. cloves
1 c. brown sugar	1/2 tsp. allspice

Dip tomatoes in boiling water to loosen skins. Peel, quarter and remove stems and seeds. Chop onions and peppers. Put all vegetables through grinder, using fine blade. Combine vinegar, sugar, Tabasco and salt in saucepan. Put in vegetables and bring to a boil. Reduce heat and cook slowly, about 2 hours, until thick, stirring occasionally. Skim off foam. Put in spices and cook about 15 more minutes. Pour into hot sterile jars and seal. Makes about 4 pints.

*

SPICED PEACHES

2 qt. small peaches	1 c. cider vinegar
Whole cloves	4-inch stick cinnamon,
2 1/2 c. brown sugar	broken

Scald peaches and peel. Stick each with a clove. Bring sugar, vinegar and cinnamon to a boil. Add fruit and cook until tender, about 10 minutes. Pack in hot sterile jars, adding syrup to within 1/2-inch of top. Seal. Makes 4 pints.

*

SPICED CANTALOUPE

3 lbs. cantaloupe, cut	1 pt. cider vinegar
in small squares	3 sticks cinnamon
2 tsp. alum	1 Tbsp. whole cloves
2 qt. water	1 tsp. allspice
3 c. sugar	

Bring alum and water to a boil. Add cantaloupe and cook 15 minutes. Drain well. Combine remaining ingredients. Add cantaloupe and cook over low heat until fruit is transparent, about 45 minutes. Put in hot, sterile jars and seal. Makes about 4 pints.

*

SPICED PLUMS

3 lbs. purple plums	8 whole cloves
1 lb. sugar	1 c. cider vinegar
2 cinnamon sticks, broken	

Prick each plum in several places with a needle. Place in a large pan. Combine remaining ingredients and bring to a boil. Pour boiling liquid over plums. Let stand 20 minutes. Drain liquid and boil again. Pour over plums again. Let stand 20 minutes. Drain and boil liquid once more. Add plums and let boil 5 minutes. Ladle into hot sterile jars. Let stand 4 weeks before using. Makes 2-1/2 pints.

*

OLD FASHIONED APPLE BUTTER

5 lbs. tart apples	3 tsp. cinnamon
3 c. apple cider	1 tsp. cloves
4 c. sugar	

Wash, peel, quarter and core apples. Bring apples and cider to a boil in heavy saucepan. Reduce heat and simmer, covered, for 20-25 minutes. Puree apple mixture in a blender. Add sugar and spices, mixing well. Pour puree into a shallow baking dish and bake at 300 degrees for 2 hours, or until thick enough to hold its shape. Pour into hot sterile jars and seal. Makes about 10 6-oz. jars.

*

RASPBERRY JAM

3 c. raspberries	1/4 c. bottle fruit
3 c. sugar	pectin

Crush berries and mix with sugar. Let stand 20 minutes. Stir in pectin and fill hot sterile jars with jam. Seal. Let stand at room temperature overnight. Store in refrigerator or freezer. Makes about 4 8-oz. jars.

*

PLUM JAM

4 c. purple plums, pitted	3 1/2 c. sugar
	1 tsp. lemon juice

Chop plums. Mix all ingredients together and let stand 1 hour. Cook until thick, stirring once in a while to prevent sticking. Pour into hot sterile jars and seal. Makes about 6 8-oz. jars.

*

STRAWBERRY JAM

4 c. strawberries,   7 c. sugar
  sliced   1 Tbsp. lemon juice

Combine all ingredients and let stand overnight. Bring to a boil, stirring often. Cook until syrup is thick. Skim off foam. Ladle into hot sterile jars and seal. Makes about 4 8-oz. jars.

*

RHUBARB-STRAWBERRY JAM

5 c. rhubarb, diced   1 3-oz. box strawberry
4 c. sugar   gelatin

Let the rhubarb and sugar stand overnight, stirring often. In the morning, boil 10 minutes. Add gelatin and mix well. Pour into hot sterile jars. Store in refrigerator or freezer. Makes about 6 8-oz. jars.

*

MINT JELLY

1 c. water   3 1/2 c. sugar
1/2 c. vinegar   3 drops green food
1/2 c. mint leaves   coloring
                  1/2 bottle fruit pectin

Heat first 5 ingredients to a boil. Add pectin and bring to a rolling boil for 1 minute. Strain out leaves. Pour jelly into hot sterile jars and seal. Makes 6 6-oz. jars.

*

RASPBERRY SAUCE

1 pt. raspberries	1 Tbsp. cornstarch
1/4 c. water	1/2 tsp. lemon juice
1/4 c. sugar	

Mash berries and strain out seeds through a sieve. Put berries in saucepan with remaining ingredients. Cook over medium heat until thick, stirring constantly. Makes about 1 cup.

*

CANTALOUPE SAUCE

1 cantaloupe, cut in	Lemon juice
small squares	Sugar

Puree cantaloupe in blender. Add lemon juice and sugar to taste. Chill.

*

CHERRY SAUCE

1/2 c. sugar	2 c. pitted tart cherries
1 Tbsp. cornstarch	1 Tbsp. butter
1/2 c. water	1 Tbsp. lemon juice
1/8 tsp. salt	

Cook sugar, cornstarch, water and salt over low heat for 5 minutes, stirring constantly. Add remaining ingredients and cook until thick and hot. Makes about 3 cups.

*

PEACH SAUCE

4 peaches   4 Tbsp. sugar

Peel and slice peaches. Mix with sugar and let stand 30 minutes. Serve over ice cream, cake or pudding. Makes about 3 cups.

*

BLUEBERRY SAUCE

1/2 c. sugar   Dash salt
1 Tbsp. cornstarch   2 c. blueberries

Mix all ingredients together and cook over low heat, stirring until syrup is thick and clear. Makes about 2 cups.

*

MINT SAUCE

1 c. mint leaves   1/2 c. boiling water
3 Tbsp. sugar   1/2 c. white vinegar

Crush mint leaves and mix with sugar. Pour boiling water over and stir until sugar is dissolved. Pour in vinegar and let steep about 1 hour. Serve with lamb. Makes about 1-1/2 cups.

*

ONION SAUCE

1/2 c. onion, chopped   1 c. milk
1 Tbsp. butter   1/2 tsp. salt
1 Tbsp. flour   Dash pepper

Cook onion in butter until yellow. Blend in flour and stir in milk slowly. Cook over low heat stirring constantly, until thickened. Add seasonings. Serve over vegetables. Makes 1 cup.

*

HERB BUTTER

1/2 lb. butter	1 Tbsp. marjoram
2 tsp. lemon juice	1 Tbsp. basil

Beat butter until light and fluffy. Add lemon juice and herbs. Makes 1 cup. (Spread on French bread, corn-on-the-cob, vegetables, broiled meat or fish.)

*

HONEY BUTTER

1/2 lb. butter	1/2 c. honey

Beat butter until light and fluffy. Gradually add honey, beating until smooth. Makes 1 1/2 cups. (Serve on biscuits, pancakes, waffles and bread.)

*

GARLIC BUTTER

1/2 lb. butter	4 cloves garlic, crushed

Beat butter until light and fluffy. Combine with garlic. Makes 1 cup.

*

De Zwaan, 200-year-old Dutch Windmill in Holland

soups

salads

BEAN SOUP

1 lb. navy beans	2 onions, chopped
2 qt. water	1/2 tsp. salt
1 large smoked ham hock	Dash pepper
1 c. celery, diced	

Cover beans with water and soak overnight. Add remaining ingredients. Cover and simmer 3-4 hours. Remove ham bone and cut meat off into soup. Serves 6.

*

CELERY SOUP

2 c. celery, cut in 1-inch pieces	2 c. milk
2 Tbsp. onion, chopped	2 envelopes instant chicken broth & seasoning
Butter	

Saute celery and onion in a small amount of butter until crispy-tender. Stir in milk and broth mix. Heat until hot and bubbly. Serves 4.

*

VEGETABLE-BARLEY SOUP

1/2 c. barley	1 c. canned tomatoes
Meaty soupbone	1/2 c. carrots, diced
2 qt. water	1 c. green beans
1/2 c. onion, chopped	1 c. potatoes, diced
1 c. celery & leaves, chopped	1 tsp. salt
	Dash pepper

Place barley, soupbone and water in large pot. Bring to a boil. Reduce heat, cover and simmer 2-3 hours. Cut meat off the bone and remove bone. Add vegetables, salt and pepper. Cook slowly until vegetables are tender--about 40 minutes. Makes about 2-1/2 quarts.

*

CUCUMBER SOUP

4 c. cucumber, peeled, seeded & sliced	6 c. chicken broth
1 medium onion, chopped	1 egg yolk
2 Tbsp. butter	1 c. half-and-half
3 Tbsp. flour	Chives, chopped

Mix vegetables together in small bowl. Melt butter in heavy pot, add vegetables and cook until golden, not brown. Sprinkle in flour and stir until blended. Stir in broth and bring to a boil. Reduce heat and simmer 10 minutes. Pour into blender, 1 cup at a time, and whirl until well blended. Return to pot. In a small bowl, beat egg yolk and cream. Add a cup of the hot soup gradually to cream mixture, stirring all the while. Return to pot and remove from heat. Sprinkle with chopped chives. Serves 6.

*

POTATO SOUP

2 c. potatoes, pared & sliced thin	1 Tbsp. butter
1/4 c. onion, minced	1/4 tsp. Worcestershire sauce
1 c. water	1 tsp. salt
1 1/2 c. milk	Dash pepper

Cook potatoes and onion in water until tender. Mash potatoes slightly with a fork. Add remaining ingredients and heat. Serves 4.

*

SALMON CHOWDER

1 c. potatoes, diced	1 lb. salmon fillet
1 c. water	1 c. milk
3 bacon slices, cut up	Salt & pepper
1 medium onion, chopped	2 Tbsp. parsley, chopped

Cook potatoes in water 10-15 minutes. Fry bacon 3-4 minutes. Add onion and cook until tender. Add bacon, onion, bacon grease and fish to potatoes and water. Cook slowly until fish is flaky and potatoes are done, about 10 minutes. Add milk, salt and pepper. Sprinkle with parsley. Serves 4.

*

TOMATO SOUP

1 pt. tomatoes, peeled	1 stalk celery
2 c. water	1/4 tsp. baking soda
1/2 tsp. onion salt	2 c. milk
Dash Tabasco	2 Tbsp. flour
	2 Tbsp. water

Boil tomatoes and water in saucepan. Add onion salt, Tabasco and celery. Simmer 15 minutes. Strain. Add the soda and let the foam die down. Add milk. Mix the flour and water together in a cup and add to the soup. Bring almost to the boiling point, stirring constantly. Cook 5 minutes. Serves 6.

*

PEAR-CHEESE SALAD

4 pears, peeled, halved & cored	2 Tbsp. mayonnaise
1 3-oz. pkg. cream cheese	2 Tbsp. chopped walnuts
	Lettuce

Stuff pear halves with a mixture of cream cheese, mayonnaise and walnuts. Serve on beds of lettuce. Serves 4.

*

GREEN GRAPE WALDORF SALAD

2 c. apples, diced
1/2 tsp. lemon juice
1 c. seedless green
  grapes

1 c. celery, diced
1/2 c. chopped walnuts
1/2 c. mayonnaise
1/2 c. whipped cream

Sprinkle lemon juice on apples and mix. Add grapes, celery and walnuts, combining well. Stir in mayonnaise and whipped cream. Serves 6.

*

COLE SLAW

3 c. cabbage
1/4 green pepper, grated
1 carrot, grated
2 Tbsp. cider vinegar

1 Tbsp. sugar
1/3 c. mayonnaise
1 tsp. onion salt
1/2 tsp. celery seed

Mix all vegetables together and sprinkle with vinegar. Combine other ingredients. Pour over vegetables and stir well. Serves 6.

*

HOT POTATO SALAD

4 medium potatoes
4 bacon slices
1 small onion, chopped
1 Tbsp. flour
1 tsp. dry mustard
1 tsp. salt

1 Tbsp. sugar
Dash pepper
1/2 c. water
1 egg, beaten
1/4 c. cider vinegar

Peel and slice potatoes. Cook in boiling salted water until tender. Drain. Cook bacon until crisp. Drain on paper towels and break into small pieces. Using 2 tablespoons of the bacon fat, cook onion until golden brown. Blend in flour, mustard, salt, sugar and pepper. Stir in the water and boil 2 minutes. Add 2 tablespoons of the hot mixture to the beaten egg and mix. Pour back into sauce. Add vinegar and reheat. Pour over the hot potatoes and mix in the chopped bacon. Serves 4.

*

DEVILED EGGS

6 eggs, hard-boiled & halved	1 tsp. prepared mustard
1/4 c. mayonnaise	1/2 tsp. salt
1 tsp. cider vinegar	Paprika

Scoop out egg yolks and mash with mayonnaise, vinegar, mustard and salt. Pile back into egg whites and sprinkle with paprika. Makes 12 halves.

*

WILTED LETTUCE

1 large head lettuce	3 Tbsp. sugar
6 slices bacon	1/2 tsp. salt
1/2 c. cider vinegar	Dash pepper
1/4 c. water	

Separate lettuce into leaves. Wash, drain and put into large bowl. Cover and refrigerate. Dice and cook bacon in skillet, saving fat. Remove and drain bacon on paper towels. In the skillet, put 1/4 cup of bacon fat and remaining ingredients. Heat until boiling. Stir in bacon. Pour over lettuce and toss lightly. Serves 6.

*

TOSSED SOYBEAN SALAD

3 c. soybean sprouts	1/4 tsp. pepper
1/4 c. salad oil	1/4 c. green peppers, chopped
2 Tbsp. vinegar	
2 Tbsp. soy sauce	1/8 tsp. garlic powder
1 tsp. sugar	2 Tbsp. sesame seeds
1/4 tsp. salt	

Place sprouts in salad bowl. Mix other ingredients together and pour over sprouts. Toss. Chill, stirring occasionally. Serves 6.

*

SWEET AND SOUR CARROT SALAD

2 lb. carrots, sliced & cooked
1 green pepper, sliced
2 medium onions, sliced
1/4 c. salad oil
3/4 c. vinegar
1 c. sugar

1 10 1/2-oz. can tomato soup
1 tsp. Worcestershire sauce
1 tsp. prepared mustard
1/4 tsp. garlic powder
1 tsp. salt
1/4 tsp. pepper

Place carrots, pepper and onions in bowl. Heat oil, vinegar and sugar in saucepan and stir until sugar is melted. Add soup and spices, mixing well. Pour over vegetables and mix. Refrigerate for a day. Serves 8.

*

MARINATED BEAN SALAD

1 1/2 c. green beans, cooked
1 1/2 c. kidney beans, cooked
1 1/2 c. wax beans, cooked
1/2 c. celery, sliced

1/3 c. sweet pickle relish
3/4 c. sugar
2/3 c. vinegar
1/3 c. salad oil
1/2 tsp. garlic powder
1 tsp. salt
1 tsp. pepper

Mix beans with celery and relish in a large bowl. Shake other ingredients together in a glass jar. Pour over vegetables and chill. Serves 8.

*

MARINATED CAULIFLOWER

1 medium cauliflower
1/8 tsp. pepper
1/4 tsp. oregano
1/4 tsp. sugar

1/8 tsp. garlic powder
4 Tbsp. salad oil
2 Tbsp. wine vinegar

Separate cauliflower into flowerets and cook in salted water until crispy-tender, about 8-10 minutes. Drain. Put remaining ingredients in glass jar and shake well. Pour over cauliflower and mix. Chill 4 hours, stirring occasionally. Serves 4.

MARINATED ASPARAGUS TIPS

1 lb. fresh asparagus	1/8 tsp. garlic powder
1/2 c. salad oil	1/2 tsp. salt
3 Tbsp. wine vinegar	1 tsp. Worcestershire
1 Tbsp. lemon juice	sauce
1/2 tsp. dry mustard	1 tsp. sugar

Snap asparagus stalks to find tender parts. Cook in salted water 10-15 minutes. Drain. Combine remaining ingredients in glass jar, shaking well. Pour over asparagus. Refrigerate 4 hours, stirring occasionally. Drain. Serves 4.

*

CUCUMBERS IN SOUR CREAM

3 large cucumbers	1 c. sour cream
1 medium onion	1 1/2 Tbsp. white vinegar
3 Tbsp. salt	Dash pepper

Slice cucumbers and onion very thin. Mix remaining ingredients together and pour over vegetables. Chill. Serves 4.

*

CUCUMBER SALAD

1 large cucumber	1 tsp. salt
1 medium tomato	Dash pepper
1/2 c. sugar	2 Tbsp. parsley,
1/2 c. white vinegar	chopped

Slice cucumber and tomato very thin. Mix remaining ingredients and pour over vegetables. Chill. Serves 4.

*

FROSTED GREEN GRAPES

Beat 1 egg white until fluffy. Dip small clusters of grapes into it and roll gently in sugar, coating evenly. Chill until dry. Use as garnish on salads or desserts.

*

main dishes

THE PASTY

Upper Peninsula Cornish miners are credited with bringing one of the most delicious dishes to Michigan with the pasty (rhymes with nasty). This meat and vegetable turnover was stuffed inside the miners' shirts--so the story goes--to keep them warm on their walks to the mine. Deep inside the copper and iron mines at dinner time, the workers could reheat this nourishing, stick-to-their-ribs meal on a shovel over a miner's lamp with no fuss or bother. It was a handy, neat way to deal with a meal.

Today pasty stands dot the roadways in U.P. mining country doing a sell-out business to tourists who have discovered this great food. With one of these wonderful meat pies, a quart of milk and a patch of grass, you're ready for a picnic.

The pasty, brought to the U.P. in the 1870s and '80s, is immortalized in a poem written in Cornish dialect. It goes:

> "I dearly love a pasty;
> A 'ot leaky one,
> With mayt, turmit and taty,
> H'onyon and parsley in 'un.
>
> The crus' be made weth suet,
> Shaped like a 'alf moon,
> Crinkly h'edges, freshly baked,
> 'E es always gone too soon."

If you're wondering, mayt means meat, turmit turnips, taty potatoes and h'onyon onions.

Quite frankly, I think my own poem says it just as well.

> There's nothing better than a pasty
> All steamy, fresh and hot.
> No, there's nothing better than a pasty
> Unless it's two you've got.

UPPER PENINSULA PASTY

4 c. flour
2 tsp. salt
1/2 tsp. baking powder
1 1/2 c. beef suet, ground
  twice
10 Tbsp. ice water
1 lb. sirloin, diced
1/2 lb. lean pork, diced

5 potatoes, peeled &
  chopped
3 turnips, scraped &
  diced
1 large onion
1 Tbsp. salt
1 tsp. pepper
Butter

In a large bowl, combine flour, salt, baking powder and suet. Mix well, using fingers, until mixture resembles coarse meal. Pour in ice water and gather into a ball. Add more water if necessary. Divide dough into six balls, dust each with flour and wrap in plastic wrap. Refrigerate for 1 hour. Combine remaining ingredients, except butter. Roll each ball of dough in a circle on a floured surface to 1/4-inch thickness. Place 1 1/2 cups filling on each over half the dough. Dot with butter. Fold over unfilled side of dough and crimp the edges, sealing by moistening lightly. The pasties look like half moons. Place on baking sheets and bake at 400 degrees for 45 minutes. Makes 6.

*   *   *

POT ROAST IN RED WINE

3 c. dry red wine
1 c. water
1 Tbsp. lemon juice
2 c. sliced onion
2 c. sliced carrots
2 cloves garlic,
  minced
1/4 tsp. dried thyme
1/2 tsp. dried parsley

1 tsp. salt
1/4 tsp. pepper
5-lb. pot roast
2 Tbsp. salad oil
1 10 1/2-oz. can cream
  of mushroom soup
1 8-oz. can tomato sauce
3 Tbsp. cornstarch
3 Tbsp. cold water

Mix wine, water, lemon juice, carrots, garlic, thyme, parsley, salt and pepper for marinade. Pour over meat in a bowl. Cover and refrigerate over- night, turning once or twice. Take meat out, saving marinade, and dry with paper towels. Brown in hot oil in heavy pot. Drain off fat. Add marinade, soup and tomato sauce. Cover and bring to a boil. Simmer until tender, about 2-3 hours. Remove meat. Stir cornstarch into water and stir into simmering marinade. Cook, stirring constantly, until thick. Strain over meat for gravy. Serves 12.

*

RED FLANNEL HASH

2 c. chopped cooked
  corned beef
2 c. cooked potatoes,
  chopped
1 c. cooked beets,
  chopped

1/4 c. onion, chopped
1/4 c. milk
Salt
Pepper
3 Tbsp. butter

Mix all ingredients together, except butter. Melt butter in skillet. Spread hash evenly in pan and cook slowly, covered, until browned on the bottom, about 30 minutes. Fold and turn out on serving dish. Serves 4.

*

OVEN FRIED CHICKEN

1 chicken, cut up	1/2 tsp. pepper
1 c. flour	2 tsp. paprika
2 tsp. salt	1/2 c. salad oil

Put flour, salt, pepper and paprika in paper bag and shake to mix. Drop chicken pieces in one by one and shake to coat. Place in salad oil poured in baking dish. Turn pieces to coat with oil. Bake, skin side down, at 400 degrees for 45 minutes. Turn chicken, skin side up, and bake 45 minutes more. Serves 4.

*

STUFFED GREEN PEPPERS

4 green peppers	1/2 c. cheese, grated
1 c. cooked rice	1/4 tsp. salt
1/4 c. chili sauce	

Cut stem ends out of peppers and remove seeds. Boil 5 minutes in salted water. Drain. Mix remaining ingredients together. Fill peppers and place in a 1/2-inch of hot water in baking dish. Bake at 350 degrees until peppers are tender, about 30 minutes. Serves 4. (If you want, add 1/2 lb. cooked ground beef to mixture.)

*

MAPLE BAKED HAM

2-inch-thick slice smoked ham	2 Tbsp. dry mustard
10 whole cloves	1/2 c. maple syrup
	1/2 c. apple cider

Stick cloves into fat on ham and rub mustard over side of it. Place in baking dish and pour a mixture of syrup and cider over the top. Bake at 350 degrees for 1 1/2 to 2 hours. Serves 6.

*

BAKED SPARERIBS AND SAUERKRAUT

3 lbs. spareribs   1 c. tomato juice
3 1/2 c. sauerkraut

Place ribs in botton of roasting pan and cover with sauerkraut. Pour tomato juice over top. Bake, covered, at 350 degrees for 3 hours. Serves 4-6.

*

BARBECUED PORK CHOPS

6 pork chops   1 Tbsp. Worcestershire
1/4 c. flour   sauce
1/4 c. vinegar   1/2 c. catsup
1/2 tsp. salt   2 Tbsp. brown sugar
1/2 tsp. dry mustard   1/4 tsp. Tabasco
1 tsp. celery seed

Coat chops with flour and brown in skillet. Stir remaining ingredients together in small bowl. Pour over the chops, cover and simmer over low heat until chops are tender and well-cooked. Serves 6.

*

ROAST PORK LOIN

3-5 lb. pork loin roast   2 tsp. garlic salt
4 tsp. dry mustard   1/4 tsp. pepper

Place pork loin in roasting pan and rub with dry ingredients. Insert meat thermometer in center of thickest part of meat. Roast, uncovered, at 350 degrees for 2-3 hours, or when thermometer reads 185 degrees. Serves 6-10.

*

BEEF STEW

1 lb. beef stew meat	1 c. tomatoes, cooked
6 Tbsp. flour	2 c. water
1 tsp. salt	3 medium potatoes, diced
1/4 tsp. pepper	6 carrots, diced
4 Tbsp. salad oil	1 turnip, diced
1 small onion,	3 stalks celery &
chopped	leaves, diced

Coat meat with flour, salt and pepper. Brown in oil. Add onion and brown quickly. Add tomatoes and water. Bring to a boil. Cover, lower heat and simmer until meat is tender, about 2 hours. Add vegetables and cook 20-30 minutes. Serves 4-6.

*

SHEPHERD'S PIE

2 lbs. ground beef	1 10 1/2-oz. can tomato
1 medium onion, chopped	soup
Salad oil	2 c. green beans
Seasoned salt	3 c. mashed potatoes
Pepper	1/2 c. cheese, grated
	Paprika

Brown ground beef and onion together in a little oil. Season with salt and pepper. Drain off fat. Stir in tomato soup. Place meat mixture in lightly greased baking dish. Put green beans on top. Spread mashed potatoes over it all. Bake at 350 degrees for 20 minutes. Sprinkle with cheese and a dash of paprika. Return to oven for another 5 minutes. Serves 8.

*

CHICKEN IN WINE

1 chicken, cut up	1/2 pkg. dry onion soup mix
1 10 1/2-oz. can cream of	1/4 tsp. thyme
mushroom soup	1/2 c. white wine

Place chicken pieces in baking dish. Mix other ingredients together and pour over chicken. Bake at 350 degrees for 1 hour. Serves 4.

STEWED CHICKEN AND DUMPLINGS

1 stewing chicken, cut up	1/4 tsp. pepper
3 c. water	1 c. flour
1 small onion, diced	2 tsp. baking powder
2 carrots, diced	2 tsp. parsley, minced
2 tsp. salt	1/4 tsp. thyme
	1/2 c. milk

Put chicken, water, onion, carrots, salt and pepper in a large pot. Cover and bring to a boil. Reduce heat and simmer 2 hours. For dumplings, mix flour, baking powder, salt, parsley, thyme and milk in a small bowl. Drop dumplings into simmering (not boiling) broth around chicken. Cover tightly for 20 minutes--don't peek. Make gravy, if you wish, by straining broth into saucepan. Combine 1/2 c. flour with 1 c. water and stir into broth. Cook until thick. Serves 4.

*

CHICKEN PAPRIKA

2 chickens, cut up	1/2 c. onions, chopped
1 tsp. salt	2 c. chicken broth
1/4 tsp. pepper	2 Tbsp. paprika
1/4 c. flour	1/2 c. sherry
1/8 tsp. garlic powder	1/2 c. sour cream
1/2 c. butter	

Coat chicken pieces with mixture of salt, pepper, flour and garlic powder. Brown in butter 10 minutes. Add onions and cook 2-3 minutes more. Add broth and paprika. Cover and cook 45 minutes. Place chicken in large baking dish. Pour sherry into broth mixture and stir well. Pour over chicken. Bake at 400 degrees for 30 minutes. Place chicken on serving platter. Stir sour cream into pan liquid and serve for gravy. Serves 6-8.

*

MICHIGAN BAKED BEANS

2 lbs. navy beans	1/2 c. vinegar
Cold water	1/3 c. catsup
2 tsp. baking soda	1/3 c. molasses
Hot water	1/3 c. prepared mustard
2 Tbsp. salt	1 small onion, chopped
2 c. sugar	1/4 lb. bacon, cut up

Soak beans overnight in cold water. In the morning cover and bring to a simmer slowly, adding more water if necessary. When beans have nearly doubled in size, stir in soda and bring to a boil. Pour off the green liquid and put beans in a colander to drain. Run hot tap water over them to clean off soda water. Wash out the pot and put beans back in. Cover with hot water and add the salt. Cover and simmer until done, about 1-1 1/2 hours. When the beans are done, strain off the juice (save for soup) and put beans in a large mixing bowl. Add the sugar, vinegar, catsup, molasses, mustard and onion, stirring well. Fill a 2 quart bean pot and another small dish--enough to take to a neighbor or friend. Cover top of beans with bacon. Bake at 350 degrees about 1-1/2 hours.

(Many thanks to my dear mother-in-law, Mrs. Helen Eberly, for sharing her great family recipe with me. She makes her baked beans with a handful of this and a pinch of that but was kind enough to translate it all into standard measurements. By the way, her baked beans are promptly gobbled up at picnics, holiday get-togethers, family reunions, etc. I think you'll discover why when you make them.)

*

BAKED BEAN SANDWICHES

Bread	Chili sauce
Baked beans	Cheddar cheese, grated

Spread bread with beans and top with chili sauce and cheese. Broil until cheese melts.

*

BAKED BEANS AND FRANKS

2 c. cooked navy beans
1 lb. frankfurters,
  split lengthwise
1 onion, chopped

1 c. tomato sauce
1/4 tsp. dry mustard
2 Tbsp. brown sugar
1 tsp. Worcestershire
  sauce

Layers beans and franks in greased baking dish. Mix other ingredients and pour over beans and franks. Cover and bake at 350 degrees for 45 minutes. Serves 4-6.

*

MACARONI AND CHEESE

3 Tbsp. butter
3 Tbsp. flour
1/4 tsp. dry mustard
2 c. milk
1/2 tsp. salt

1/4 c. onion, chopped
2 c. sharp cheese
4 c. cooked macaroni
Paprika

Melt butter and stir in flour and mustard. Add milk, stirring over low heat until thick. Stir in salt, onion and 1 1/2 cups cheese until cheese is melted. Mix sauce with macaroni and pour into greased baking dish. Sprinkle with rest of cheese and a dash of paprika. Bake at 350 degrees about 35-40 minutes. Serves 6.

*

CHEESE PUDDING

6 slices bread
Butter
1/4 lb. sharp cheese,
  grated

2 eggs, beaten
1 c. milk

Spread bread with butter on both sides and cube. Sprinkle cheese over bread. Pour eggs and milk over cubes and mix well. Place in greased baking dish and refrigerate 3 hours or overnight. Bake at 275 degrees for 45 minutes. Serves 4.

*

LAMB STEW

1 lb. lean lamb, cut in cubes	Water
Salt	2 potatoes, diced
Pepper	4 carrots, diced
Flour	4 stalks celery with leaves, diced
1 onion, sliced	1 turnip, diced
2 Tbsp. salad oil	1 Tbsp. parsley, chopped

Sprinkle meat with salt, pepper and flour. Brown with the onion in hot oil. Add water to cover. Cover and cook slowly until meat is almost done, about 1-1/2 hours. Add potatoes, carrots, celery and turnip. Cook until tender, about 20-30 minutes. Add parsley. Serves 4.

*

PAN-BROILED LAMB CHOPS

Loin, rib or shoulder chops	Salt
Salad oil	Pepper

Place chops in a hot, heavy skilled that has been lightly greased with oil. Brown quickly on both sides. Turn chops on sides to brown the fat. Reduce heat and cook slowly, turning often. Do not add water and do not cover. From time to time, pour off excess fat. Chops 3/4 to 1-inch-thick take 10-15 minutes to cook. Season with salt and pepper before serving.

*

LAMBURGERS

1 lb. ground lamb	1/2 c. dry bread crumbs
1/4 c. onion, minced	1 egg
1 Tbsp. parsley, chopped	1 tsp. seasoned salt
	1/4 tsp. pepper

Mix all ingredients together and refrigerate 1 hour. Shape into 6 patties and fry in skillet.

*

TURKEY TETRAZZINI

2 Tbsp. butter
1 Tbsp. flour
1 10 1/2-oz. can cream
  of mushroom soup
1 c. milk
1/4 tsp. salt

1/2 tsp. marjoram
2 c. cooked turkey,
  diced
1 4-oz. can mushrooms
1/2 lb. spaghetti, cooked
1 c. cheddar cheese,
  grated

Melt butter in saucepan. Stir in flour, soup, milk and seasoning. Cook, stirring constantly, until thick. Mix turkey and mushrooms into sauce. Put spaghetti in bottom of baking dish. Pour turkey mixture over top. Sprinkle with cheese. Bake at 400 degrees for 20 minutes. Serves 4.

*

TURKEY CASSEROLE

1 10-oz. pkg. frozen
  broccoli spears
2 c. seasoned
  stuffing cubes
4 c. cooked turkey,
  sliced

2 10 1/2-oz. cans cream
  of mushroom soup
1/2 c. sherry
1 c. chicken broth
1/2 c. cheddar cheese,
  grated

Cook broccoli according to package directions. Place 1 cup stuffing in bottom of greased baking dish. Put broccoli spears on top. Place turkey slices on top. Mix soup, sherry and broth together. Pour over turkey. Sprinkle stuffing on top. Sprinkle cheese over all. Bake at 350 degrees for 45 minutes. Serves 8.

*

fish & game

WHAT IS A WOLVERINE?

Michigan is named the Wolverine State in spite of the fact that the only wolverines around are in zoos. Wolverines are vicious, nasty little creatures with few redeeming qualities--something Michiganders would just as soon ignore.

Numerous attempts have been made in the state legislature to change Michigan's "pet" animal to, among others, the beaver or timber wolf. However, the tenacious wolverine manages to hang on and all attempts to knock him from his top spot in Michigan in more than 100 years have met with defeat.

A Wolverine?

Davy Crockett came up with his own description of the people from the Wolverine State in his 1845 Almanac. He said:

"The chaps from the Wolverine State are the all-greediest, ugliest an sourest characters on all Uncle Sam's 26 farms. They are in thar nature, like their wolfish namesakes, always so etarnal hungry that they bite at the air and hang their underlips and show the harrow teeth of their mouths as if they'd jump right into you an swaller you hull, without salt. They are, in fact, half wolf, half man and 'tother half saw mill.

"I met a Wolverine one day in the forest who had just swallowed a buck, an that war only enough to start his appetite, an make him al ravenous. He turned up his eyes at me an opened his airthquake jaws as if he war goin to chop off my head without axin. I chucked a lamb or two at him, but it war no more use than a hoss-fly to a buzzard.

"'Mr. Wolverine,' says I, 'you stare at me with a reg'lar cannibal grin, but darn me if you mustn't fight before you can bite; my name's Crockett and i'm an airthquake.' And if the critter didn't draw up his under-lip and fall to eaten off the bark of a tree while his eyes watered along with his mouth, then take my whiskers for wolfskins."

It's a wonder anyone set foot in Michigan again!

*　　　　*　　　　*

LAKE SUPERIOR WHITEFISH AMANDINE

4 large whitefish, cleaned	2 Tbsp. butter
Flour	1/4 c. almonds, blanched & slivered
2 Tbsp. salad oil	1 Tbsp. lemon juice

Coat whitefish with flour and fry in oil and butter until brown on both sides. Remove to serving platter. Add almonds to fat and cook until brown. Stir in lemon juice and pour over fish. Serves 4.

*

BARBECUED WHITEFISH

1 whole whitefish, dressed	Salt
Salad oil	Pepper
	1 Tbsp. lemon juice

Brush both sides of fish with oil. Place in shallow pan and season with salt and pepper. Pour lemon juice over fish and let stand 30-60 minutes. Place on greased grill and cook about 15 minutes. Cover loosely with aluminum foil and cook for another 10 minutes. Each pound serves 2 persons.

*

FRIED PIKE WITH TOMATOES

4 pike fillets	1/4 tsp. pepper
1/3 c. flour	1/3 c. butter
2 tsp. tarragon	3 tomatoes, cut in wedges
1 tsp. salt	1 tsp. capers

Dip fillets in mixture of flour, tarragon, salt and pepper. Heat butter in large skillet and fry fillets until golden. Turn and move to side of skillet. Put tomatoes in skillet and sprinkle fish with capers. Cook until tomatoes are hot and fish is flakey. Serves 4.

*

BROILED TROUT IN HERB SAUCE

2 lbs. trout, dressed	1/2 tsp. cumin
3 Tbsp. butter	1/4 tsp. salt
1/8 tsp. garlic powder	2 Tbsp. vinegar
2 green onions, minced	2 Tbsp. water
1 Tbsp. dried parsley	

Split fish down the back. Place on greased broiler rack, skin side up. Brush with butter. Broil 5-8 minutes, or until brown. Baste with fat. Turn, baste other side, and broil until brown. Meanwhile, combine remaining ingredients in a small bowl. Serve over broiled fish. Serves 4.

*

SALMON STEAK IN MUSTARD SAUCE

1 2-lb. salmon steak	Salt
1 Tbsp. salad oil	Pepper
1 Tbsp. flour	1/4 c. crumbs
1/2 tsp. dry mustard	1 Tbsp. butter
3/4 c. milk	

Place steaks in shallow greased pan. In a saucepan blend oil, flour and mustard. Stir in the milk and cook, stirring until thickened. Add salt and pepper. Pour sauce over fish and sprinkle with crumbs. Dot with butter. Bake at 350 degrees for 35-40 minutes. Serves 4.

*

PAN FRIED PIKE

4 pike fillets	1 Tbsp. water
Salt	1 egg, beaten
Pepper	Fine bread crumbs
Flour	Salad oil

Season fillets with salt and pepper. Roll in flour. Beat water and egg together. Dip fish in egg, then roll in crumbs. Heat about 1/8-inch oil in skillet and fry the fish slowly until brown on one side. Turn and brown the other side. Serves 4.

*

BAKED TROUT FILLETS

2 Tbsp. butter	Pepper
1 lb. trout fillets	Dash paprika
Flour	1 Tbsp. lemon juice
Salt	

Melt 1 tablespoon of butter and place in shallow baking dish. Lightly flour fillets and place, skin side down, in dish. Season with salt, pepper and paprika. Sprinkle lemon juice over fish. Dot with rest of the butter. Bake at 350 degrees for 15-20 minutes. Serves 3-4.

*

VENISON IN SOUR CREAM

3 c. red wine, divided	1 6-1b. venison roast
1/2 c. apple cider	Salt
2 bay leaves	1/4 c. butter
4 whole peppercorns	2 Tbsp. flour
1 Tbsp. parsley, chopped	1 c. sour cream

In a shallow pan combine 2-1/2 cups wine, cider, bay leaves, peppercorns and parsley. Place venison in mixture, cover and refrigerate overnight, turning occasionally. Remove venison from mixture and place on roasting pan rack, fat side up. Sprinkle with salt and insert meat thermometer in center of meat. Melt butter. Strain 1 cup of marinade and add to the butter. Brush meat with the mixture. Roast at 325 degrees for 2-1/2 to 3 hours. Baste with butter marinade often. Remove roast to serving dish and keep warm. In a saucepan mix flour and a dash of salt. Add 1 cup drippings from venison and stir until smooth. Stir in 1/2 cup wine and cook over medium heat, stirring constantly, until smooth and thick. Reduce heat and stir in sour cream. Serve over venison. Serves 8-10.

*

MARINATED VENISON

3 lbs. sliced venison, flank, breast or shoulder	1 Tbsp. chopped parsley
	1 clove garlic, crushed
	1 tsp. peppercorns
1/4 c. salad oil	1 bay leaf
1 c. red wine	3 Tbsp. salad oil
2 Tbsp. lemon juice	1 Tbsp. flour

Marinate meat overnight in the oil, wine, lemon juice, parsley, garlic, peppercorns and bay leaf. Spoon mixture over meat often. Drain the meat, saving marinade. Brown in oil and place meat in casserole dish. Stir flour into skillet and cook for a minute. Add the marinade, stirring until hot and bubbly. Pour over venison and bake at 350 degrees for 40 minutes. Serves 6.

*

ROAST BEAR PAWS

2 large bear paws, skinned	1 tsp. salt
1 c. flour	1/2 tsp. pepper
3 Tbsp. shortening	2 onions, sliced thin
1 tsp. cinnamon	4 slices bacon
1 tsp. allspice	1/2 c. water
	1/2 c. tomato juice

Dust paws with flour and brown in shortening. Remove to a casserole dish and sprinkle with seasonings. Cook onions in shortening until tender. Place onions around paws and lay bacon on top. Pour water and tomato juice over paws. Bake, covered, at 350 degrees for 4 hours. Serves 4. (If you catch the whole bear, double the recipe for four bear paws.)

*

PHEASANT A LA KING

1 6-oz. can mushrooms	2 tsp. flour
1/2 c. green pepper, chopped	1 c. milk
1/4 c. celery, chopped	1 tsp. salt
2 Tbsp. butter	1/4 tsp. pepper
1 10 1/2-oz. can cream of chicken soup	1/4 c. pimiento, chopped
	2 c. pheasant, cooked & diced

Drain mushrooms, reserving liquid. In skillet, cook green pepper and celery in butter until tender. Stir in mushroom liquid and soup. Stir flour into milk to blend and pour into skillet. Simmer, stirring to blend flour. Add mushrooms and remaining ingredients. Cook until hot. Serve on toast or pastry shells. Serves 6.

*

ROAST ORANGE DUCK

1 duck	6 Tbsp. currant jelly
Salt	1/4 tsp. dry mustard
Onions, quartered	1/4 tsp. salt
Apples, quartered	1 c. orange juice
5 Tbsp. butter, divided	1/2 tsp. grated orange peel

Rub inside of duck with salt. Stuff loosely with onions and apples. Truss. Place breast side up on rack in baking pan. Melt butter and baste duck with 2 tablespoons of it. Roast at 350 degrees for 40-45 minutes per pound. In the meantime, combine remaining melted butter and other ingredients over low heat, stirring until well blended. Baste duck with mixture every 15-20 minutes. Serves 2.

*

RABBIT STEW

1 rabbit, dressed & cut up	2 tsp. salt
2 c. vinegar	1/4 tsp. pepper
2 c. water	3 medium onions, sliced
1/2 c. sugar	3 Tbsp. butter
1 medium onion, sliced	1 Tbsp. flour
4 whole cloves	4 carrots, cut up
2 bay leaves	2 potatoes, cut up
1/4 tsp. basil	Red wine
	2 Tbsp. flour
	2 Tbsp. water

Place rabbit pieces in a marinade of vinegar, water, sugar, onion, cloves, bay leaves, basil, salt and pepper. Refrigerate 2 days, turning often. Fry onions in butter. Add flour, blending well. Remove rabbit from marinade and dry. Place in skillet with onions and brown. Add carrots, potatoes and enough wine to cover. Cover and simmer about 30 minutes, or until the meat is tender. Mix flour and water together. Pour into stew and cook to thicken gravy. Serves 4.

*

Old Presque Isle Light House

vegetables

ASPARAGUS HOLLANDAISE

1 lb. asparagus
3 egg yolks
2 Tbsp. lemon juice

1/2 tsp. salt
Dash pepper
1/2 c. melted butter

Snap asparagus stalks. Cook, covered, in salted water 10-15 minutes. Mix egg yolks, lemon juice, salt and pepper in blender for 5 seconds. Add in butter while blending again for 5 seconds more. Heat in double boiler over low heat. Place asparagus on serving dish and pour sauce over. Serves 4.

*

SAUTEED ASPARAGUS

1 lb. asparagus
1/4 c. butter
Dash salt

Dash pepper
Dash rosemary
1 tsp. lemon juice

Slice asparagus stalks slantwise about 1/2-inch-thick. Leave tips whole. Melt butter in skillet until bubbly. Add asparagus, salt, pepper and rosemary. Stir asparagus while it cooks over medium-high heat until crispy-tender, about 3-5 minutes. Remove from heat and stir in lemon juice. Serves 4.

*

GREEN BEANS AND TOMATOES

1 Tbsp. salad oil
1 Tbsp. onion,
  chopped
1/3 c. green pepper,
  chopped

1 c. cooked tomatoes
1 1/2 c. cooked green
  beans
1/4 tsp. salt
Dash pepper
1/2 c. croutons

Heat oil in skillet and brown onion and green pepper. Add tomatoes and cook for 5 minutes. Add beans, salt and pepper. Cook 10 minutes. Turn into serving dish and top with croutons. Serves 4.

*

BEETS IN SOUR CREAM

2 c. raw beets, grated	1/4 tsp. salt
4 Tbsp. butter	3 Tbsp. lemon juice
1/4 tsp. sugar	1/2 c. sour cream

Combine beets, butter, sugar, salt and lemon juice in saucepan. Cover and cook 20 minutes, stirring occasionally. Stir in sour cream. Serves 4.

*

HARVARD BEETS

6 Tbsp. sugar	1/2 c. water
4 Tbsp. flour	4 1/2 c. cooked beets,
1/2 tsp. salt	diced
1/2 c. vinegar	2 Tbsp. butter

Mix sugar, flour and salt together in saucepan. Gradually add the vinegar and water, stirring well, over medium heat. Bring to boiling point, stirring constantly. Add beets and mix well. Add butter. Serves 6.

*

PICKLED BEETS

4 1/2 c. cooked beets, sliced	1/2 c. vinegar
1 medium onion, sliced	4 Tbsp. sugar
1/2 c. water	1/2 tsp. salt

Place beets and onion in a bowl and mix. Combine water, vinegar, sugar and salt in saucepan and bring to a boil. Pour vinegar mixture over beets. Cover and refrigerate overnight. Serve cold. Serves 6.

*

CARAWAY CABBAGE

1 small cabbage,
  cooked, cut
  in wedges
2 Tbsp. butter
1/3 c. vinegar
	1/2 tsp. caraway seeds
	1 tsp. sugar
	1/4 tsp. salt
	1/2 c. sour cream

Place cabbage on serving dish and keep warm. Heat butter, vinegar, caraway seeds, sugar and salt in saucepan. When hot and well blended, stir in sour cream and remove from heat. Pour sauce over cabbage. Serves 4.

*

SAUERKRAUT

20 lbs. cabbage	1/2 lb. coarse salt

Shred cabbage. Layer with salt in a large ceramic crock, starting with cabbage and ending with salt. Cover with a clean cloth. Weight it down with a plate and a big rock. Keep cabbage at temperature below 60 degrees but above 40 degrees. Remove scum daily and place a clean cloth, plate and rock back on cabbage. Let stand for at least a month. To can, heat sauerkraut to 180 degrees and pack firmly in hot sterile jars. Add juice to within 1/2-inch of top. Seal and process. (Sauerkraut also freezes well by simply putting it in freezer bags in the freezer.) Makes about 8 quarts.

*

CELERY CASSEROLE

4 c. celery, cut in
  1-inch pieces
1/2 c. water
1 10 1/2-oz. can cream
  of chicken soup

2 Tbsp. pimientos,
  chopped
1 c. mild cheese, grated
1/2 c. walnuts
1/2 c. bread crumbs

Cook celery in water 8 minutes. Drain. In baking dish mix celery, soup, pimientos and cheese. Mix walnuts and bread crumbs together. Sprinkle over top. Bake at 350 degrees for 30 minutes. Serves 6.

*

BRAISED CELERY

4 c. celery, sliced
1/2 c. water
1/4 tsp. salt

1/2 tsp. dried basil
Dash garlic powder
1/4 tsp. salt

Simmer celery in water until crispy-tender, about 5 minutes. Drain. Stir in seasonings. Serves 4.

*

CAULIFLOWER AU GRATIN

1 medium cauliflower,
  cooked
2 Tbsp. butter
2 Tbsp. flour

1/2 c. cheese, grated
1/2 tsp. salt
1 c. milk
1/4 c. bread crumbs

Place cauliflower in greased baking dish. In saucepan, melt butter and stir in flour to make a smooth paste. Slowly add milk, cooking over medium heat and stirring constantly. When thick, add cheese and salt. Stir until well blended. Pour over cauliflower and sprinkle crumbs over top. Bake at 350 degrees for 20 minutes. Serves 4.

*

MAPLE BAKED CARROTS

8 large carrots   2 Tbsp. brown sugar
2 Tbsp. maple syrup   2 Tbsp. butter

Cut carrots into 2-inch pieces. Cook, covered, 15 minutes. Drain. Place in greased baking dish. Pour syrup and sugar on top. Dot with butter. Bake at 375 degrees for 20 minutes. Stir once or twice. Serves 4.

*

CORN AND CHEESE CASSEROLE

1/3 c. bread cubes   3/4 c. cheese, grated
1 1/2 c. cream-style corn   1/2 tsp. salt
2 tsp. onion, minced   2 eggs, well beaten
2 tsp. green pepper,   1/2 c. hot milk
   chopped   Dash pepper

Blend all ingredients together. Pour into a greased baking dish set in a pan of hot water. Bake at 350 degrees for 1 hour. Serves 4.

*

CORN PUDDING

3 eggs   1 tsp. salt
1 1/3 c. warm milk   1/2 small onion, chopped
3 Tbsp. butter   2 c. cooked corn
1 Tbsp. sugar

Put eggs in blender and whirl for 5 seconds. Add remaining ingredients and blend 10 seconds. Pour into greased baking dish and bake at 350 degrees for 1 hour. Serves 4.

GREEN PEPPERS AND TOMATOES

1/2 c. onions, chopped	1/2 tsp. dried basil
1 Tbsp. salad oil	1 Tbsp. flour
2 c. cooked tomatoes	4 large green peppers,
1/4 tsp. garlic powder	cut in 1-inch strips
1 tsp. salt	2 Tbsp. salad oil

Saute onions in oil until tender. Add tomatoes, garlic powder, salt, basil and flour. Cook over medium-low heat, uncovered, until sauce thickens, about 10 minutes. Saute green peppers in salad oil until crispy-tender, about 3-4 minutes. Place in serving dish and pour tomato sauce over top. Serves 4-6.

*

BAKED ONIONS AND CHEESE

4 medium onions	2 Tbsp. butter
1/4 tsp. salt	1/2 c. sharp cheese,
1/8 tsp. pepper	grated
Water	1/2 c. bread crumbs

Cut onions in half crosswise and place in baking dish. Sprinkle with salt and pepper. Pour in enough water to cover bottom of dish. Dot with butter. Cover and bake at 375 degrees for 30 minutes. Top with a mixture of the cheese and bread crumbs. Return to oven and bake uncovered 10 minutes longer. Serves 4.

*

MUSHROOM HUNTING IN MICHIGAN

In May, when the oak leaves are as big as squirrels' ears and the apple trees blossom, mushroom hunters go slightly crazy in Michigan.

Morels, shaped like miniature Christmas trees, lure thousands of pickers to forest, stream, grove and farmland areas. It's not an uncommon sight to see dozens of cars parked along side the road for no apparent reason. A closer inspection will reveal mushroom hunters, like busy ants, scouring the land for the tasty treats.

There is a real art to the hunt and serious mushroomers do not take their hobby lightly. Persons have been known to travel hundreds of miles to a locale in search of that certain batch with unbeatable flavor. Maps are printed showing good picking place. Fellow hunters whisper locations of choice spots. Rumors are rampant about where the picking's best--many started by veterans to get novices out of their territory.

A number of communities, including Mesick, Boyne City, Gaylord, Harrison and Lewiston, hold annual mushroom festivals, many with guide services, instructions on which mushrooms to eat and prizes for the biggest and best.

Here are a few recipes to try after you get your big haul.

DRIED MUSHROOMS

Using a needle and thread, string the mushrooms from stem through the top. Hang in the sun for a few days. Bring inside and hang in the kitchen for two or three weeks until dry. They'll be handy there for snipping off when you need them. To use, just soak in enough hot water to cover for a few minutes. Squeeze out the excess water and they're ready to use. Save the soaking water for soup or gravy.

*

STEAMED MUSHROOMS

1 lb. mushrooms, cut in half	1/8 tsp. pepper
1 tsp. seasoned salt	1/2 c. butter
1/4 tsp. paprika	2 Tbsp. sherry
	2 Tbsp. chopped parsley

Put mushrooms on a 24x18-inch piece of aluminum foil. Sprinkle with salt, paprika and pepper. Dot with butter and sprinkle with sherry. Seal up foil, leaving some room for expansion. Place in shallow pan and bake at 400 degrees for 20 minutes. Sprinkle with parsley. Serves 6.

*

PICKLED MUSHROOMS

3 lbs. mushrooms	2 Tbsp. salt
1 1/2 c. sliced onion	2 cloves garlic, crushed
4 c. wine vinegar	3 bay leaves
2 c. water	1 tsp. dried thyme
2 Tbsp. dill seed	3 Tbsp. dried parsley

Bring all ingredients to a boil in large pan. Reduce heat and simmer 5 minutes. Pack in hot, sterile jars. Seal. Makes 3 quarts.

*

SAUTEED MUSHROOMS

2 lbs. mushroom caps	Dash pepper
1/4 c. butter	1 tsp. lemon juice
1/2 tsp. salt	

Saute mushrooms in butter, salt and pepper until tender. Cook until liquid evaporates. Stir in lemon juice and serve. Serves 6.

*

FRIED ONION RINGS

1 c. flour	4 medium onions, sliced
1 c. beer, room	1/4-inch-thick
temperature	Salt
Salad oil	

Sift flour into a bowl and make a well in the center. Slowly pour in beer and stir gently until smooth. Let batter rest for 3 hours at room temperature. Heat oil to 365 degrees in deep fryer or saucepan. Dip onion slices into batter. Fry in oil 2-3 minutes, or until golden brown. Place on paper towels to drain. Sprinkle with salt. Serves 4.

*

POTATOES AU GRATIN

3 medium potatoes,	1/4 tsp. pepper
pared and sliced	1 c. hot milk
1 Tbsp. flour	1 Tbsp. butter
1 tsp. salt	1/2 c. cheese, grated

Place a layer of potatoes in a greased baking dish. Top with a sprinkling of flour, salt and pepper. Repeat until all the potatoes are used. Pour milk over potatoes and dot with butter. Cover and bake at 350 degrees for 30 minutes. Remove cover and continue baking another 20 minutes. Sprinkle cheese over top and bake for 10 more minutes. Serves 4.

*

SQUASH AND SOUR CREAM

1 tsp. seasoned salt
1/4 tsp. celery seed
1 c. sour cream

4 c. cooked acorn squash,
   cut in 2-inch squares
1/2 tsp. dill seed

Mix seasoned salt and celery seed in sour cream. Pour over squash in serving dish. Sprinkle with dill seed. Serves 4-6.

*

WHIPPED SQUASH

4 c. hubbard squash,
   cut in 2-inch pieces
1 tsp. salt

1 Tbsp. butter
1 Tbsp. brown sugar
2 Tbsp. evaporated milk

Cook squash for 25 minutes. Drain. Mash and mix in remaining ingredients. Beat with mixer until creamy. Serves 4-6.

*

ZUCCHINI CASSEROLE

2 c. zucchini,
   sliced thin
1 tomato, sliced
   thin

1 onion, sliced thin
1/2 c. mozzarella
   cheese, grated
1/4 tsp. oregano

Layer half the zucchini, tomato and onion in greased baking dish. Sprinkle with half the cheese and all the oregano. Repeat, ending with cheese. Bake uncovered at 350 degrees for 40 minutes. Cover and bake 20 minutes more. Serves 4.

*

MAKING MAPLE SYRUP
(From "Between the Iron and the Pine")*

by Lewis C. Reimann

Maple syrup and maple candymaking was a spring activity we all looked forward to and we all enjoyed. After a long winter, it was a frolic to get out in the sugar bush, to see the first signs of spring in the melting snow, the squirrels frisking in the treetops at the first peep of the sun, the calling of the bright bluejays and the budding of the trees.

Sugaring was no easy task. It required long preparation. It necessitated the construction of a roof or shed under which a long stone fireplace was built to hold the long, wide pan for boiling the sap. Great piles of wood were cut by hand and hauled in. Dozens of sap buckets of every conceivable size, ranging from five pound lard pails to five gallon wooden water pails were saved all year. Holes were bored with brace and bit into the sugar maple tree trunks waist high on the sunny side and the containers hung from grooved spiles driven into the holes, with the groove uppermost to catch the sap as it came from the hole and dropped into the bucket.

It takes about fifty gallons of sap to make a gallon of syrup. A steady, slow heat was required to evaporate it. If the fire was too hot or the amount of sap in the pan too thin, the syrup burned and became useless except for stock feed.

---

*"Between the Iron and the Pine," published in 1952, is one of a number of colorful and witty books written by Mr. Reimann about the Upper Peninsula's mining and lumbering days. This particular book is about his pioneer family and its life around the turn of the century.

It took one person's full time to feed and
watch the fire and stir the sap, while others
carried the sap in buckets hung from neckyokes or
hauled it in with a team and sled in barrels.

Anyone who complains at the price of maple syrup
should spend a spring in the sugar bush to appreciate
the amount of work and time it takes to produce one
gallon. Perhaps the only reason a person will spend
many hours tapping, stirring, firing and processing
syrup and then sell it for a few dollars a gallon
is that just getting out of doors after a long,
dreary winter offers an exhilaration which is part
of the compensation.

Sugaring off is the most exciting part of the
process. When the sap is boiled down to a certain
consistency, a spoonful is poured on a patch of
clean, white snow. If it hardens to a satisfactory
degree it is pronounced ready for canning. It is
at that time the workers gather around for the
tasting of the result.

The weather must be watched for successful syrup
making. Frosty nights and warm days assure a good
run of sap. The frost stops the formation of buds
while the warm sun sends the sap up from the roots.
Warm nights and warm days spell the end of the run.

The hard work of sugar bushing is forgotten on
cold winter mornings when nut brown pancakes come
direct from the hot kitchen stove to be drowned
with golden maple syrup, or when baking powder
biscuits are served at dinner with fresh homemade
butter and our own maple syrup.

In the spring, woodsmen and farmers tap maple trees and use the sap as a drink in place of water. The liquid has just enough sugar and maple flavor to make it a delicious and satisfying drink. Men working in the woods usually had a few sap buckets hung from the maple trees around them. The sap was thought to have a medicinal virtue--a sort of spring tonic like sulphur and molasses.

*   *   *

Fallasburg Bridge near Grand Rapids

breads
pancakes

BEER RYE BREAD

5 c. unbleached flour	1 Tbsp. instant coffee
4 c. rye flour	1/4 c. butter
2 c. milk	1 1/4 c. beer, at room
2 tsp. salt	temperature
1/3 c. molasses	2 pkgs. dry yeast
1 pkg. brown gravy mix	2 Tbsp. caraway seeds

Mix flours in a bowl. Scald milk and stir in
salt, molasses, gravy seasoning, coffee and butter.
Cool. Pour beer into a large bowl. Sprinkle in
yeast and stir until dissolved. Stir in lukewarm
milk mixture, caraway seed and 4 cups flour. Beat
until smooth. Mix in 2 more cups flour. Turn out
onto floured board and knead in remaining flour
until dough is smooth, about 10 minutes. Place in
greased bowl, turning once to grease top. Cover
and let rise in warm place 1 hour. Punch down and
divide in half. Shape each half into a ball.
Place each ball on a greased baking sheet and shape
into a mound. Cover and let rise in warm place
until almost double, about 50 minutes. Put in a
COLD* oven and set temperature at 375 degrees.
Bake for about 45 minutes. Makes 2 loaves.

*

*Placing yeast breads in a cold oven just before
they have risen to the tops of their baking pans or
before they have doubled virtually assures well-
risen loaves of bread. The bread rises as the
temperature in the oven does. Compensate for the
slow baking temperature by adding about 10 minutes
to the baking time of bread recipes.

COTTAGE CHEESE DILL BREAD

1 pkg. dry yeast	2 Tbsp. dill seed
1/4 c. warm water	2 tsp. salt
1 c. cottage cheese	1/4 tsp. baking soda
1/4 c. shortening	1 egg, beaten
2 Tbsp. sugar	2 1/2 c. flour
1 Tbsp. minced onion	

Soften yeast in water. Warm cottage cheese in saucepan. Stir in shortening, sugar, onion, dill seed, salt, baking soda and yeast. Beat in egg. Add flour, a little at a time, to make a soft dough. Knead on floured board until smooth, about 10 minutes. Put in greased bowl, turning once to grease top. Cover with towel and let rise in warm place 1 hour. Punch down. Cover and let rest 10 minutes. Place in greased loaf pan. Cover and let rise again until almost double, 30-45 minutes. Put in COLD oven and bake at 350 degrees for about 50 minutes. Makes 1 loaf.

*

HONEY WHEAT BREAD

4 pkgs. dry yeast	1/4 c. salad oil
2 1/2 c. warm water	1/2 c. honey
2 Tbsp. sugar	3 c. unbleached flour
1 Tbsp. salt	5 c. whole wheat flour

Dissolve yeast in water and let stand. In large bowl, mix together sugar, salt, oil and honey. Add water and yeast. Beat in unbleached flour until smooth. Gradually add whole wheat flour. Place on a lightly floured board and let rest, covered, for 10 minutes. Knead until smooth, about 10 minutes. Place in a large, greased bowl. Turn to grease top surface. Cover and let rise in warm place until double, about 1 hour. Punch down and let rest 10 minutes. Put dough into 2 greased loaf pans. Cover and let rise again until almost double, about 45 minutes. Put in COLD oven and bake for 45-50 minutes at 400 degrees. Makes 2 loaves.

*

APPLE BREAD

1/2 c. shortening
1 c. sugar
1 1/2 Tbsp. buttermilk
2 eggs
1 tsp. vanilla
1 tsp. baking soda
1 tsp. salt

1 c. cider
2 c. flour
1 1/2 c. apples, chopped
1/2 c. walnuts, chopped
2 tsp. sugar
1/2 tsp. cinnamon

Cream shortening and sugar. Add buttermilk, eggs and vanilla, blending well. Alternate adding dry ingredients with cider. Stir in apples and walnuts. Pour into a loaf pan. Sprinkle with a mixture of sugar and cinnamon. Bake at 350 degrees for 1 hour and 15 minutes. Makes 1 loaf.

*

RHUBARB BREAD

2 1/2 c. flour
1 tsp. salt
1 tsp. baking soda
1 1/2 c. brown sugar
1 egg, beaten

1/2 tsp. vanilla
2/3 c. salad oil
1 c. sour milk
2 c. rhubarb, diced
1/2 c. chopped nuts

Sift together flour, salt, soda and sugar. Beat egg, vanilla and salad oil. Stir in milk. Blend into sifted ingredients. Stir in rhubarb and nuts. Pour into 2 greased loaf pans. Sprinkle with topping. Bake at 325 degrees for 60 minutes. Makes 2 loaves.

TOPPING

1/2 c. brown sugar

1 Tbsp. butter

*

PUMPKIN BREAD

3 c. flour
2 tsp. baking soda
1/2 tsp. baking powder
1 tsp. cinnamon
1 tsp. cloves
1 tsp. salt
1/2 c. butter

1 c. sugar
1 1/2 c. brown sugar
4 eggs
2 c. cooked pumpkin
1/2 c. water
1/2 c. chopped walnuts
1/2 c. raisins

Sift together flour, soda, baking powder and spices. In a large mixing bowl, cream butter and sugar. Beat in eggs and stir in pumpkin. Alternate adding flour with water about 3 times until all is used. Stir in walnuts and raisins. Pour batter into 2 greased loaf pans. Bake at 350 degrees for 50-60 minutes. Makes 2 loaves.

*

ZUCCHINI BREAD

3 c. flour
1 1/2 c. sugar
3/4 tsp. baking soda
1 tsp. baking powder
1 tsp. salt
1 tsp. cinnamon

1/2 tsp. nutmeg
2 c. shredded, unpeeled
  zucchini
1 c. chopped nuts
1/2 c. raisins
3 eggs
1 c. salad oil

Combine flour, sugar, soda, baking powder, salt, cinnamon, nutmeg, zucchini, nuts and raisins. In another bowl beat eggs and oil. Pour into flour mixture and stir until blended. Bake at 350 degrees for 1-1/2 hours. Cool in pan 10 minutes before turning out.

*

COTTAGE CHEESE PANCAKES

1 1/2 c. cottage cheese	1/2 tsp. salt
6 eggs	1/2 c. flour
1 Tbsp. salad oil	1/4 tsp. baking powder

Beat cottage cheese until smooth. Beat in eggs. Mix in oil, salt, flour and baking powder. Bake on lightly greased griddle. Makes about 12 pancakes.

*

WHOLE WHEAT PANCAKES

1 c. whole wheat flour	1/4 tsp. salt
2 Tbsp. sugar	1 egg
3 tsp. baking powder	1 c. buttermilk
1/2 tsp. baking soda	2 Tbsp. salad oil

Blend dry ingredients well. In a separate bowl beat egg and mix in buttermilk and oil. Add to dry ingredients, mixing well. Fry on hot greased griddle. Makes about 8 pancakes.

*

BLUEBERRY WAFFLES

2 eggs, well beaten	3 tsp. baking powder
1 c. milk	1 tsp. salt
1/4 c. salad oil	1 Tbsp. sugar
2 c. flour	1 c. blueberries

Add the milk and oil to eggs and mix well. Combine dry ingredients and add to liquids. Gently fold in blueberries and bake in waffle iron. Makes about 8 waffles.

*

BLUEBERRY MUFFINS

2 1/2 c. flour
2 1/2 tsp. baking powder
1/4 tsp. salt
3/4 c. sugar, divided

1 c. buttermilk
2 eggs, beaten
1/2 c. salad oil
1 1/2 c. blueberries

Sift together the flour, baking powder, salt and 1/2 cup sugar. Add buttermilk, eggs and oil, mixing only until dry ingredients are dampened. Gently fold in berries. Spoon into greased muffin tins, filling 2/3 full. Sprinkle with remaining sugar. Bake at 400 degrees for 20-25 minutes. Makes about 16.

*

CHEESE POPOVERS

2 eggs
1 c. milk
1 c. flour

1/4 tsp. salt
1/2 c. cheddar cheese,
    grated

Beat eggs, milk, flour and salt for 2 minutes. Pour into 6 large greased custard cups that were first heated in the oven. Sprinkle with cheese. Bake at 425 degrees for 40 minutes. Makes 6.

*

POTATO DOUGHNUTS

1 c. mashed potatoes
1 Tbsp. salad oil
2 eggs
1/2 c. milk
2 1/2 c. flour

1/2 c. sugar
1/2 tsp. salt
1 Tbsp. baking powder
1/8 tsp. nutmeg
1/4 tsp. cinnamon

Beat together potatoes, salad oil, eggs and milk. Sift remaining ingredients together and add to potatoes. Divide dough into 2 pieces. Roll out on floured board to 3/4-inch thickness. Cut with doughnut cutter and fry in oil at 365 degrees until golden brown. Drain on paper towels. Dust with powdered sugar. Makes 12-18.

*

SOYBEAN BROWN BREAD

1 1/2 c. soy flour	2 tsp. baking soda
1 1/2 c. whole wheat flour	1/2 tsp. salt
1 c. yellow cornmeal	2 c. buttermilk
1/2 c. sugar	1 c. molasses
	1 c. raisins

Mix flours, cornmeal and sugar together. Stir soda and salt into buttermilk. Stir buttermilk mixture into flours. Add molasses. Stir in raisins. Pour into 5 16-oz. greased fruit or vegetable cans. Cover tightly with foil. Place on a rack in a large kettle. Add boiling water around cans to a 2-inch depth. Cover kettle and cook slowly for 1 hour, keeping water just below boiling point. Makes 5 loaves, 6 slices each.

*

SOURDOUGH STARTER

2 c. flour	2 c. warm water
1 pkg. dry yeast	

Combine all ingredients well in a glass or pottery bowl--DO NOT use a metal one. Let stand in a warm place for 48 hours, stirring occasionally. When it's yeasty smelling and bubbly, pour into a glass or pottery jar to store in the refrigerator. Before using, let starter stand in a warm place (a warm oven that has been turned off is ideal) until mixture is bubbly, about 3 hours. If starter separates, just stir before using. Replace the starter with 1 cup flour and 1 cup water for every cup of mixture you remove. The starter should be used at least once every 2 weeks to keep it going well.

*

SOURDOUGH BREAD

1 c. starter	1 Tbsp. salt
3 c. flour	1 tsp. baking soda
2 c. warm water	3-3 1/2 c. flour
3 Tbsp. sugar	Melted butter

Combine starter, flour, water, sugar, salt and soda in a large glass or pottery bowl--do not use metal. Beat until smooth. Cover with waxed paper and let stand in warm place overnight. Mix in enough flour to make a stiff dough. Knead on a floured board until smooth and satiny, about 10 minutes. Shape dough on greased baking sheets into 2 loaves. Brush with butter. Cover and let rise in warm place until almost double, about 1 1/2-2 hours. Place in COLD oven and bake at 375 degrees for 50-55 minutes. Makes 2 loaves.

Doesn't rise very high.

*

SOURDOUGH PANCAKES

1 c. starter	2 Tbsp. melted butter
2 1/2 c. flour	1/3 c. milk
2 c. warm water	2 eggs, separated
1 tsp. baking soda	3 Tbsp. sugar
1 tsp. warm water	

Combine starter, water and flour. Let stand overnight. Mix soda in warm water and stir into starter with butter, milk, egg yolks and sugar. Beat egg white until stiff peaks are formed. Fold into pancake batter. Let batter rest for 10 minutes. Fry on hot greased griddle. Makes about 16 pancakes.

*

VINEGAR PIE
(From "Vinegar Pie and Other Tales")*

By Al Barnes

So you, Mrs. Modern Housewife, think you had a rough day? You struggled out of bed at the obnoxious hour of 8:30 a.m. and plugged in the electric percolator and the electric toaster. You opened the front door a wee bit and snatched up the quart of milk and the morning paper.

At 9:30 you turned off the electric dishwasher, ran the last of the kitchen refuse through the garbage grinder, turned on the radio or television and took five to recoupe your shattered nerves.

After a day like that, who wouldn't be worn in body, be crabby and snarling at hubby, and bark at the youngsters.

But things were different back in the 19th century when Mrs. Frank Flarity, Manistee, cooked in the lumber camps of the Grand Traverse region. In those roaring days a lumberjack worked from sunup to sundown and was always ready for supper call.

Mrs. Flarity began her day at 5:30, when she cooked for the Buckley and Douglas Lumbering Company at Twin Mountain camp, Nessen City. Three times a day she prepared a meal for 65 healthy appetitès. Of course she had a couple of flunkies, sometimes called "cookees" by the fellows who write romantic pieces about the camps.

---

*"Vinegar Pie and Other Tales" is a collection of anecdotes and lively stories about the pioneers and history of the Grand Traverse region. Mr. Barnes, who published the book in 1959, is an historian, freelance writer and veteran newspaperman--many of the tales first appearing in his column for the Traverse City Record-Eagle.

Twice each week she baked 35 loaves of bread and 350 buns. Every forenoon she baked a 50-pound keg of molasses cookies and a 50-pound keg of white cookies. (The kegs were probably former nail containers.) Every other day of the week she turned out a key of fried cakes and every morning before daylight she had 18 pies out of the oven.

For 20 years, she followed the camps. She boiled and baked enough beans to feed a small navy. Side pork and beef steak were common bill-of-fare and now and then a little venison--there was always lots of meat in the camps where she worked.

Breakfast in a lumber camp was one to bolster a weakened constitution. "Most generally," Ms. Flarity has said, "we had warmed up 'taters and salt pork for breakfast, along with all the pancakes the men could eat. And coffee for breakfast, lots of it, boiled in a big pot and poured black and scalding hot."

"You know," she remarks, "there's more to warming up 'taters than most women know. You have to get the meat fryings just so hot--almost smoking--before the 'taters are put in the iron skillet. Then you chop them with a tin can until they are pretty fine. Brown them and turn them two or three times and they are fine, not at all like the soggy ones you get in a restaurant."

Dessert? Of course! There was always an ample supply of prune pie, raisin pie, dried apple pie and, once in a while, a little lemon pie if the cook could get some lemon extract.

There were no recipes to go by when one cooked for a lumber camp. One just took a pinch of this and a scoop of that, a little fat for shortening, and a dab of something else and--presto!--good, wholesome food.

One of the most colorful cooks of the region was Mrs. Mary Conklin, Traverse City. She went to work as a flunky on a wannigan at the age of 12.

To the boys of the pine, a wannigan was a woods scow--a floating eating house. The first wannigan on which Mrs. Conklin worked ferried between Elk Rapids and Eastport, tending the appetites of the crews cutting for the famous Dexter and Noble firm.

The appetites of the seagoing lumberjacks were no different. It was the same story. A bushel of cookies baked before daylight; thousands of fried cakes; beans, bacon, fat salt pork from a barrel--all staples of the lumber era.

Another item of which the men were fond was cornmeal mush. For breakfast, it served as a cereal. One cooks it slow and thin and serves it with milk and brown sugar. One can also cook it a little longer, pour it in a bread pan and let it cool, then slice and fry it crispy brown. With a dab of butter and a bit of maple syrup, it is a dish for a king.

From yeast to oven, Mrs. Conklin, like scores of other cooks through the northland, provided her own ingredients for baking. Wheat was milled in local establishments, and she raised her own hops. In recalling the use of yeast in those early days, she said it was "kept alive," as long as two years. "You just take some boiled 'taters,'" she explained, "jam them good. You steep the hops just right and mix them, and there you have it."

The Swedish and Norwegian lumberjacks liked their thin, odorous sourdough pancakes. The worse they smelled, the better they liked them. Others liked "raise cakes"; some wanted cornmeal in the batter; and others liked buckwheat, especially in the winter because, they explained, buckwheat was "heatin'."

No story of food and appetites would be completed without mention of an old favorite! Vinegar Pie, a lumber camp standby. Is there a housewife today who could make one?

Mrs. Russell Woods, Kalkaska, cooked them for a
number of camps over the northern part of the state.
The last camp was the Tindle and Jackson camp at
Pellston.

Just in case you want to whip up a little
Vinegar Pie, here is her method:

1 1/4 c. sugar
1 1/2 c. boiling water
1/3 c. vinegar*
1/3 c. cornstarch
Dash nutmeg (if you have it)

Stir the ingredients together and cook until
clear and thick. Stir half the mixture into 3
beaten egg yolks; combine mixture again; place
entire filling back on wood range for 1 minute, add
a tablespoon of butter and pour into a baked shell.
If you wish to be fancy, just in case the girls are
going to drop in, make the usual meringue. (But
lumberjacks were happy to have the pie without the
fringe on top.)

*

The call to meals varied according to the
location of the camps, the whims of the cook, or the
will of the workmen. Sometimes a great iron triangle
struck by a heavy iron was the signal. Or, it was a
long dinner horn with a call like that of a mating
bull moose. It could have been a trumpet call
through the barrel of a 12 gauge shotgun. It could
have been the simple expedient of the lumberjacks
looking at a dollar pocket watch. One thing was
certain, no one was ever late for a meal.

Meal time was for eating. The men had their own
places at the long plank tables and they kept them.
Heaven help the new man who got in the wrong place.
There was no idle chatter at the tables. "Pass
the 'taters." "Some bread." "Hand me the butter."
That was the extent of the conversation.

Louis Nelson, Keystone (Grand Traverse County), was one of the lads who wielded the pancake turner and fired a green wood stove. He, like scores of others, was one of the "long hour" boys of the woods camps.

But the ladies, bless 'em, were in there in major numbers. They didn't have any electric toasters or dishwashers; they had no vacuum coffee makers or electric mixers.

They had ambition, endurance and skill. On top of all that, they had long hours. A 15-hour day was not unusual, but an 8-hour day was rare indeed.

Although he didn't mention it in the book, Mr. Barnes said the vinegar should be from a health store since it should be natural and not processed.

*   *   *

desserts

TRAVERSE CITY CHERRY PIE

Pastry & lattice
  top for 8-inch
  pie
3 c. pitted
  tart cherries

1 c. sugar
1/2 c. flour
4 drops almond extract
1/8 tsp. salt
1 1/2 Tbsp. butter

Mix cherries together with sugar, flour, extract and salt. Pour into pastry shell. Dot with butter. Place lattice top on, sealing with water and crimping edges high. Bake at 425 degrees for 10 minutes. Reduce heat to 350 degrees and bake 30 minutes longer.

*

BLACK CHERRY BURGUNDY PIE

1 c. water
1/4 c. sugar
1 3-oz. pkg. cherry
  gelatin
2 c. dark sweet pitted
  cherries

1 pt. vanilla ice cream
3 Tbsp. burgundy
1 tsp. lemon juice
1 9-inch baked pastry
  shell

Boil water and dissolve sugar and gelatin in it. Stir in cherries. Add ice cream by spoonfuls, stirring until melted. Blend in wine and lemon juice. Pour into pie shell and chill until set.

*

PEACH CREAM PIE

20 large marshmallows
1/4 c. milk
1/2 pt. whipping cream

3 c. fresh peaches,
  sliced
1 8-inch graham cracker
  crust pie shell

Melt marshmallows with milk in top of double boiler. Cool. Whip cream and fold into marshmallow mixture. Add peaches. Pour into crust and chill until set.

*

STRAWBERRY CREAM PIE

1 pt. strawberries, sliced	2 c. milk
1 Tbsp. sugar	2 eggs, beaten
2/3 c. sugar	1 tsp. vanilla
1/3 c. flour	1 9-inch baked pie shell
	2 c. whipped cream

Mix strawberries and sugar together and let stand. In a double boiler, combine sugar and flour. Slowly stir in milk while cooking over hot water. Stir constantly until mixture thickens. Cover and let cook without stirring for 10 minutes. Add a small amount of mixture to eggs and blend. Pour eggs into mixture and cook for 3 more minutes. Chill thoroughly. Add vanilla. Pour into pie shell. Put sliced strawberries over filling. Spread whipped cream on top.

*

APPLE PIE

Pastry for 9-inch, 2-crust pie	1 Tbsp. flour
6-7 tart apples, pared & thinly sliced	1 tsp. cinnamon
1 c. sugar	1/4 tsp. nutmeg
	1 Tbsp. lemon juice
	2 Tbsp. butter

Line pie plate with pastry. Roll out dough for top crust and set aside. Combine sugar, flour and spices. Mix apples with lemon juice. Mix all ingredients together, except butter. Fill pie shell with apple mixture and dot with butter. Cover with top crust, slashing in several places to allow steam to escape. Bake at 400 degrees for 50 to 60 minutes.

*

PUMPKIN PIE

1 9-inch unbaked
  pie shell
2 c. cooked or
  canned pumpkin
1/2 c. brown sugar
1/4 c. maple syrup
1 tsp. cinnamon

1/2 tsp. ginger
1/2 tsp. nutmeg
1/2 tsp. salt
2 eggs, slightly beaten
1 13-oz. can evaporated
  milk

Mix pumpkin, sugar, syrup and spices together. Blend in eggs and milk, stirring until smooth. Pour into pie shell and bake at 375 degrees for 50-60 minutes.

*

COTTAGE CHEESE PIE

1 1/2 c. cottage cheese
1/2 c. sugar
2 Tbsp. flour
1/4 tsp. salt
1/4 tsp. cinnamon

1 tsp. lemon juice
2 eggs, separated
2 c. milk
1 9-inch unbaked pie shell

Combine cottage cheese, sugar, flour, salt, cinnamon and lemon juice in a blender, beating until smooth. Put in egg yolks and blend. Add milk gradually, blending for a few more seconds. Beat egg whites with mixer until smooth. Fold into cottage cheese mixture. Pour into pie shell. Bake at 350 degrees for 1 hour.

*

RASPBERRY PIE

6 c. raspberries
1/2 c. water
2/3 c. sugar
3 Tbsp. cornstarch
1 9-inch baked pie shell
1 c. whipped cream

Mash berries and strain seeds out through a sieve. Place berries, water, sugar and cornstarch in saucepan and cook, stirring constantly, until thick. Cool. Pour into pie shell. Chill until set. Spread whipped cream on top before serving.

*

PEAR PIE

Pastry for 2-crust
   9-inch pie
5 pears, cored,
   peeled & sliced
3/4 c. brown sugar
Dash salt
1/4 tsp. ginger
1/4 tsp. mace
1 1/2 Tbsp. cornstarch
3 Tbsp. orange juice
1 tsp. lemon juice
1 Tbsp. butter

Place pears into pastry-lined pie plate. Combine dry ingredients and sprinkle over pears. Pour juices over mixture and dot with butter. Cover with top crust, slashing in center. Seal and flute edges. Bake at 425 degrees for 45-50 minutes.

*

RHUBARB CUSTARD

6 c. rhubarb, cut in
   1-inch pieces
2 c. sugar
1 Tbsp. butter
5 Tbsp. flour
2 tsp. nutmeg
2 eggs, beaten

Place rhubarb in 9x9-inch baking dish. Mix remaining ingredients together. Spoon over rhubarb and bake at 400 degrees for 20 minutes. Reduce heat to 350 degrees and bake for 20 more minutes. Serves 4-6.

*

CARROT CAKE

2 c. flour	1/2 tsp. lemon rind
2 c. sugar	1 tsp. salt
2 tsp. baking powder	1 1/2 c. salad oil
2 tsp. baking soda	3 c. raw carrots, grated
2 tsp. cinnamon	4 eggs
1 tsp. nutmeg	1/2 c. walnuts, chopped

Sift dry ingredients together. Combine with remaining ingredients, except walnuts, beating well. Stir in walnuts. Pour into a greased 9x13-inch pan. Bake at 325 degrees for 45 minutes. When cool, frost.

FROSTING

1 8-oz. pkg. cream cheese	2 tsp. vanilla
1 box powdered sugar	1/2 c. butter

Beat all ingredients together until fluffy.

*

TOMATO SOUP CAKE

3 c. flour	1/2 c. shortening
3 tsp. baking powder	1 c. sugar
1/2 tsp. baking soda	2 eggs, well beaten
1/2 tsp. cloves	1 10 1/2-oz. can tomato
1/2 tsp. cinnamon	soup
1/2 tsp. nutmeg	1 c. raisins

Sift flour, baking powder, soda, cloves, cinnamon and nutmeg together. Cream shortening until light and fluffy. Slowly beat in sugar. Add eggs. Mix thoroughly. Add flour mixture alternately with soup, blending until smooth. Stir in raisins. Pour into 2 greased 8-inch cake pans and bake at 375 degrees 35 minutes. Cool and frost. (See carrot cake frosting.)

*

SHERRY CAKE

1 18 1/2-oz. pkg. yellow cake mix	3/4 c. salad oil
	3/4 c. sherry
1 3 3/4-oz. pkg. instant vanilla pudding	4 eggs
	1 tsp. nutmeg

Combine all ingredients, beating well. Pour into greased bundt pan and bake at 350 degrees for 45 minutes. Cool in pan for 5 minutes before turning out on rack. Sprinkle with powdered sugar or spoon over a glaze of powdered sugar moistened with sherry.

*

HONEY APPLESAUCE CAKE

1/2 c. shortening	1 tsp. nutmeg
1 c. honey	1/4 tsp. cloves
3 c. sifted flour	1 1/2 c. applesauce
1 1/2 tsp. baking soda	1/2 c. raisins
1/2 tsp. salt	1/2 c. walnuts, chopped
1 tsp. cinnamon	Powdered sugar

Cream shortening and honey. Sift flour, soda and spices together. Beat into creamed mixture alternately with applesauce. Stir in raisins and nuts. Pour into a greased 9x13-inch pan and bake at 350 degrees for 40 minutes. Cool and cut into squares. Sprinkle with powdered sugar.

*

SOYBEAN LEMON SPONGE CAKE

2/3 c. flour	6 egg whites
2/3 c. soy flour	1/2 c. sugar
1/2 tsp. baking powder	6 egg yolks
1/2 tsp. salt	1/4 c. water
1 c. sugar	2 tsp. lemon extract
1 tsp. cream of tartar	

Mix flours, baking powder, salt and 1 cup sugar together. Add cream of tartar to egg whites and beat until soft peaks are formed. Gradually add 1/2 cup sugar, beating until stiff peaks are formed. Mix egg yolks with water and extract in a separate bowl. Stir flour mixture into yolk and beat 30 seconds. Fold into beaten egg whites. Pour batter into an ungreased tube pan. Bake 45-50 minutes until lightly browned. Invert pan on plate, but leave cake inside for at least 1 hour before removing.

*

CHERRY-CHEESE SQUARES

1/2 c. soft butter	1 3-oz. pkg. cream cheese
1 1/4 c. flour	1 lb. pitted tart cherries
2 Tbsp. sugar	3 Tbsp. cornstarch
1 3-oz. pkg. vanilla	1 c. sugar
pudding	1 Tbsp. lemon juice
1 3/4 c. milk	

Mix butter, flour and sugar together to make a dough. Pat in bottom of square baking dish and bake at 350 degrees for 10 minutes. Cool. Combine pudding mix and milk in saucepan, cooking until thick. Beat in cream cheese, blending until smooth. Cool and pour over dough. Cool in refrigerator. Mix cherries with cornstarch, sugar and lemon juice in saucepan. Cook until thick and clear. Cool. Spread over top of pudding. Serves 8.

*

CHERRIES JUBILEE

1/2 c. sugar
1/4 tsp. salt
1 Tbsp. cornstarch
1 c. water

1 lb. dark sweet
   cherries, pitted
3 Tbsp. brandy
1 pt. vanilla ice cream

Combine sugar, salt, cornstarch and water until well blended. Add cherries and cook over medium heat until thickened, stirring constantly. Pour brandy over top and ignite. Spoon immediately over ice cream. Serves 4.

*

CHERRY BATTER PUDDING

3 Tbsp. butter
2 c. sugar, separated
2 eggs
2 c. sifted flour
2 tsp. baking powder
1/4 tsp. salt

1/4 tsp. almond extract
1 c. milk
3 c. pitted tart cherries
1 1/4 c. water

Beat butter and 1/2 c. sugar. Beat in eggs. Sift flour, baking powder and salt together. Add to creamed mixture alternately with extract and milk. Pour into a greased casserole dish. Sprinkle cherries over top and cover with remaining sugar. Bring water to a boil and pour over top. Bake at 375 degrees for 45 minutes. Serves 6.

*

STRAWBERRY-CHERRY PARFAIT

Cherry ice cream
Strawberry jam
   (see page 24)

Chopped walnuts
Whipped cream

Alternate layers of ice cream and strawberry jam mixed with nuts in a tall glass. Top with whipped cream and a sprinkling of nuts.

*

STRAWBERRY SHORTCAKE

1 qt. strawberries, sliced	2 Tbsp. sugar
1 c. sugar	1/3 c. shortening
2 c. flour	3/4 c. milk
2 tsp. baking powder	Butter
1 tsp. salt	Whipped cream

Mix strawberries and sugar together. Set aside. Sift dry ingredients together. Cut in shortening and blend until mixture is crumbly. Make a well and pour in milk. Stir with a fork and gently form dough into a ball. Put on lightly floured board and knead about 15 times. Roll or pat out dough to 1/2-inch thickness. Cut into rounds with a 3-inch cutter. Spread half the round with soft butter. Top with remaining rounds. Place on a baking sheet and bake at 450 degrees for 10 to 15 minutes. Split shortcakes and spoon half the strawberries over bottom layer. Top with short-cakes and more strawberries. Add a spoonful of whipped cream on top. If desired, garnish with a few whole strawberries. Makes 6 servings.

*

PEACH CRUMBLE

1/2 c. flour	1/2 tsp. cinnamon
1/2 c. rolled oats	1/8 tsp. cloves
1/2 c. brown sugar	1/2 c. butter
1/2 c. sugar	4 c. fresh peaches, sliced
1/4 tsp. nutmeg	1 tsp. lemon juice
1/4 tsp. salt	2 Tbsp. water

Mix dry ingredients together. Stir in butter until mixture is crumbly. Put peaches in bottom of 8x8-inch baking dish. Cover with lemon juice and water. Sprinkle crumb mixture over top and pat down. Bake at 350 degrees for 45 minutes.

*

APPLE BROWN BETTY

1/3 c. brown sugar
1/2 tsp. cinnamon
1/4 tsp. salt
3 c. small bread cubes

1/3 c. melted butter
4 tart apples, peeled
& diced

Mix first 5 ingredients and put a layer in bottom of greased baking dish. Cover with a layer of apples. Continue layers until all ingredients are used. Finish with a layer of crumbs on top. Cover and bake at 375 degrees for 1 hour. Uncover the last 10 minutes to brown top. Serves 4.

*

BLUEBERRY COBBLER

3 c. blueberries
3/4 c. water
1 c. sugar
1 tsp. lemon juice
1 Tbsp. cold water

1 Tbsp. cornstarch
2 Tbsp. butter
1 c. biscuit mix
1/3 c. milk
1 Tbsp. sugar

Heat blueberries, water, sugar and lemon juice in large skillet. Mix the cornstarch in water and add to blueberries. Bring to a boil, stirring frequently. Dot with butter. Add milk and sugar to biscuit mix and drop from a tablespoon onto berries. Cover and cook over low heat 20 minutes. Serve hot with milk or ice cream. Serves 4-6.

*

GRAPE CREAM

2 c. green grapes
1/2 c. sour cream

3 Tbsp. brown sugar
1/4 tsp. ginger

Place grapes in serving bowl. Dab on cream. Mix brown sugar and ginger together. Sprinkle over cream. Serves 4.

*

MACKINAC ISLAND

Mackinac (pronounced Mackinaw) Island is a unique place in Northern Michigan where horses, bicycles and fudge reign supreme.

Since no cars are allowed on the Island, except emergency vehicles, the only way to get around is by bike, horse drawn carriage or foot. It's a strange sensation to ride a bicycle around the three-mile-long island without having to worry about getting mowed down by a frenzied motorist who's five minutes late for work. The only hazard are the calling cards left behind by the horses, but they are hurriedly whisked out of sight by street sweepers armed with shovels and buckets.

Fudge shops abound on the resort island, selling tons of candy every season to sweet-toothed tourist. You can watch the fudge being transformed from thick syrup into solid candy by white-aproned men and women who knead and turn it on long marble slabs. They make everything from basic chocolate and vanilla to such varieties as pistachio and chocolate rum nut.

Of course there are other points of interest besides bikes, horses and fudge such as Old Fort Mackinac and the Grand Hotel. But it's still great fun just to ride a bike, eat a half-pound of fudge and sit in the park watching the other tourists doing the same thing.

Here are some Island-type fudge recipes to try on a cold wintery night when a hot summer day on Mackinac is only a delicious dream.

*   *   *

VANILLA FUDGE

1/2 c. milk	Dash salt
1/2 c. butter	1 tsp. natural vanilla
1/2 c. brown sugar	extract
1/2 c. white sugar	2 c. powdered sugar

Mix milk, butter, sugars and salt in a heavy saucepan. Cook over medium heat and bring to a boil, stirring constantly. Boil 6 minutes, stirring all the while. Remove from heat. Add vanilla and powdered sugar. Beat with mixer until smooth and thick, about 6 minutes. Pour into buttered pan and freeze for 20 minutes. Cut into pieces. Makes a little more than a pound.

*

CHOCOLATE FUDGE

Follow recipe above but add 1 1-oz. square chocolate to boiling mixture.

*

PEANUT BUTTER FUDGE

Follow vanilla fudge recipe but cut butter to 1/4 cup and add 1/2 cup peanut butter.

BAKED PEARS

6 pears, unpeeled,   1/2 c. maple syrup
  halved & cored   1/2 c. water
1/2 c. brown sugar   1/4 tsp. ginger

Place pears in baking dish. Combine remaining
ingredients and pour over pears. Bake at 325
degrees for 1 hour. Add more water if needed to
deep fruit from burning. Serves 6.

*

MAPLE BAVARIAN

1 1/4 tsp. unflavored   1 c. hot maple syrup
  gelatin   1 c. whipped cream
1/3 c. cold water

Put gelatin in water and let stand 5 minutes.
Pour syrup into gelatin and stir well. Chill until
thickened. Fold in cream and chill until set.
Serves 4.

*

BAKED EGG CUSTARD

2 c. milk   1/8 tsp. salt
3 eggs, beaten   1 tsp. vanilla
1/4 c. sugar   Nutmeg

Scald milk and let cool. Blend eggs, sugar and
salt together. Stir slowly into the milk. Mix in
vanilla. Strain into 4 custard cups. Sprinkle
with nutmeg. Set cups in shallow baking pan and
pour hot water, 1-inch-deep, around. Bake at 325
degrees 40-45 minutes. Serves 4.

*

ASPARAGUS COOKIES

1 c. cooked, mashed asparagus	1 c. brown sugar
1 c. raisins	1 egg
1/2 c. asparagus water (used in cooking asparagus)	1/2 tsp. salt
	1 Tbsp. vanilla
	1 1/2 c. flour
1 c. shortening	1 tsp. baking soda
	1 1/2 c. rolled oats

Heat asparagus, raisins and water to boiling. Cover and let cool. Cream shortening, salt, vanilla, sugar and egg. Beat in flour and baking soda. Mix in cooled asparagus and raisins. Stir in oatmeal. Drop by spoonfuls on greased cookie sheet. Bake at 325 degrees 10-12 minutes. Makes about 3 dozen.

*

MINT COOKIES

1/2 c. butter	1/2 tsp. vanilla
1/2 c. sugar	1 tsp. baking powder
1 egg	1/4 tsp. salt
4 tsp. dried mint	1 c. flour

Cream butter and sugar together. Add egg, mint and vanilla, beating well. Sift dry ingredients together and stir in. Drop by spoonfuls onto greased cookie sheets. Bake at 375 degrees for 10 minutes. Makes 2 dozen.

*

MAPLE SYRUP CANDIES

2 c. powdered sugar	1 tsp. vanilla
1 c. maple syrup	1/2 tsp. lemon extract
1/2 c. evaporated milk	1 c. walnuts, chopped

Boil sugar, syrup and milk in heavy saucepan without stirring until mixture reaches 240 degrees. Remove from heat and beat with a wooden spoon until smooth. Add vanilla and lemon extract. Beat again until well blended. Stir in nuts. Drop by spoonfuls onto waxed paper and let stand 1 hour. Makes 24 pieces.

INDEX
(Listed by agricultural products)

FISH

GAME

GRAINS

GRAPES

GREEN BEANS

GREEN PEPPERS

HONEY

ICE CREAM

Although not an agricultural product, salt plays an important part in food preparation and so is included in this book. Michigan, with its vast salt deposits, has been the nation's leading producer for many years. Most salt is mined in deep caverns under Detroit where the rock salt is brought up by the ton to be turned into the white sprinkly stuff on your kitchen shelf.

ABOUT MICHIGAN

--Michigan's motto is "Si Quaeris Peninsulam
  Amoenam, Circumspice" (If you seek a pleasant
  peninsula, look about you.)

--The state tree is the white pine.

--The state flower is the apple blossom.

--The state bird is the robin.

--The state fish is the trout.

--The state stone is the Petoskey stone.

--Michigan is bordered by four of the five Great
  Lakes.

--With 3,251 miles of Great Lakes shoreline,
  Michigan has the longest freshwater coast in
  the world.

--Michigan leads the nation in the number of state
  parks and recreation areas with a total of 2,953.

--Detroit is first in receipt of shipments among
  all Great Lakes ports.

--The Sault (pronounced Soo) Ste. Marie locks handle
  more ship traffic than the Panama Canal.

--Michigan State University, founded in 1855, was
  the world's first agricultural college and the
  nation's first land-grant college.

--The University of Michigan, founded in 1817, was
  the nation's first state university.

--Beaver Island is the only place in the nation ever
  rule by a monarch, King Strang.

--Michigan has two nationally acclaimed fine
arts camps. Blue Lake Fine Arts Camp, serving
elementary through high school students, has
an enrollment of 3,000 every summer and
specializes in international exchange programs.
Interlochen National Music Camp, founded in 1928,
was one of the first camps devoted to artistically-
talented students. Van Cliburn is among its
alumni. Interlochen Fine Arts Academy, founded
in 1962, is an arts-centered school for high
school students.

--Detroit has four major sports teams with the
Detroit Tigers, the Detroit Lions, the Detroit
Red Wings, and the Detroit Pistons.

--Michigan produces about 20 automobiles a
minute in assembly lines within an 85-mile
radius of Detroit.

--Michigan's Upper Peninsula has the largest
commercial deposit of metallic copper in the
world.

--Isle Royale National Park in Lake Superior
is the nation's only island national park.
All travel on the 133,844-acre park is
limited to foot because it is a wilderness
area.

--Michigan is first among inland states in
commercial fishing.

eberly press

1004 Michigan Ave.
E. Lansing, MI 48823